MICROWAVE COOKING FOR HEALTH

Beverley Piper is a qualified home economist and cookery teacher. She lives in Ashford, Kent, where she writes her books and magazine articles and teaches microwave cookery from her own test kitchen. She also gives public demonstrations to large audiences around the country and has appeared regularly on BBC Television's *Pebble Mill At One* demonstrating microwave cooking. She has recently started up a successful catering company in partnership with two colleagues. Her other publications include *Microwave Cooking*, *Cooking in Colour – Microwave Cooking*, *Microwaving for Ones and Twos* and a series of Microwave Cookery Cards.

Beverley Piper is married with two teenage sons.

KU-191-551

MICROWAVE COOKING FOR HEALTH

Beverley Piper

PENGUIN BOOKS

Penguin Books Ltd, Harmondsworth, Middlesex, England
Viking Penguin Inc., 40 West 23rd Street, New York, New York 10010, USA
Penguin Books Australia Ltd, Ringwood, Victoria Australia
Penguin Books Canada Ltd, 2801 John Street, Markham, Ontario, Canada L3R 1B4
Penguin Books (NZ) Ltd, 182–190 Wairau Road, Auckland 10, New Zealand

First published 1987

Filmset in Century Schoolbook (Linotron 202) by
Rowland Phototypesetting Ltd,
Bury St Edmunds, Suffolk

Made and printed in Great Britain by
Cox & Wyman Ltd, Reading

For my husband, Howard,
and children, Iain and Adam,
for their constant support
and their help in tasting new recipes
at almost every meal!

CONTENTS

Introduction xi
The Microwave Oven and Healthy Eating 1
How to be a Successful Microwave Cook 7
Microwave Knowledge 9
Reheating Cooked Foods 14
Defrosting 16

RECIPES

Starters Hot And Cold

Fish

Vegetables and Salads

Main Dishes

CONTENTS

Desserts

Children's Menus

INTRODUCTION

Varying theories are offered by the experts on what should constitute a healthy diet. To try to read and follow them all would be impossible. There are certain sensible guidelines, however, and using them this book hopes to lead you, gradually, towards a healthier diet by using beneficial ingredients in the recipes and by explaining why we should avoid certain foods which may, in quantity, actually do us harm.

Most people are aware, with the publicity about high blood pressure, heart disease and cancer, that many of us need to change our diet if we are to prolong a healthy existence. Basically we should reduce our intake of fat, sugar and salt and increase our fibre intake. Proteins, vitamins, minerals and carbohydrates are necessary in varying amounts. Such a diet need not be expensive or boring, but we must be aware of the ingredients we are using and should try to avoid certain products.

A gradual approach is necessary. No one should attempt to change the eating habits of a lifetime overnight, but a gradual progression towards a more healthy diet would benefit us all.

FATS AND OIL

A high-fat diet has been closely linked with hardening of the arteries and heart disease. Fat is particularly high in calories, so a reduction in its intake should cause a weight loss which is almost always beneficial.

There are different types of fat. Butter, an animal fat, and vegetable margarine, a vegetable fat, are classic examples, both of which contain exactly the same amount of calories. When fat is to be used, those actually labelled 'high in polyunsaturates' are better than animal fats, which are rich in saturated fatty acids.

The recipes in this book use very little added fat of any sort, and because of the ability of the microwave to cook without added fat, I am confident that you will hardly notice its absence. Avoid using butter or margarine as a spread on biscuits and bread, which often taste better and are far more easily digested without it. In the recipes where some form of fat is necessary I have used polyunsaturated margarines or oils.

MEAT

Meat is one of the main sources of fat in our diet. Many people are unaware of this as often the fat is distributed throughout the meat tissue and hardly visible. Cut down on meat and use it in small amounts with other ingredients such as rice, vegetables and pulses to extend it. Substitute poultry, fish and offal such as liver and kidney for a healthier menu.

CHEESE

Cheese varies enormously in its manufacture and can be high-, medium- or low-fat. It is a wonderful ingredient in cookery and in the recipes I have mostly used medium-fat or low-fat varieties. Hard cheese such as Cheddar is high in saturated fat and salt and can be rather indigestible.

Parmesan cheese, a hard Italian cheese made from partially skimmed milk, is useful as, owing to its strong flavour, a little goes a long way. Readily available in supermarkets, it should be stored in an airtight container.

MILK

Milk is a particularly valuable food. It is a good source of protein, calcium and vitamin B. It is exceedingly versatile in cooking. I suggest simply that the change be made to semi-skimmed pasteurized milk, which has had half of its fat removed and can be delivered by the milkman or bought in the super-market.

CARBOHYDRATE

Carbohydrates can be divided into two groups – refined and unrefined. We should all increase the amount of unrefined carbohydrates in our diet, such as wholemeal bread, potatoes and pasta, as these give the body work to do in breaking them down, making us feel full, giving us energy and hopefully discouraging us from eating too many refined carbohydrates such as sugar, cakes and biscuits.

Sugar goes straight into the bloodstream and gives us a sudden feeling of energy. However, the feeling is short-lived. Sugar is linked with obesity and tooth decay and should be avoided. Small amounts of honey and dried fruits such as raisins may be used in place of sugar as they are very sweet. If sugar is necessary in a recipe, choose muscovado brown sugar as it is not refined, unlike its white-sugar counterpart.

SALT

A diet which is too high in salt has been connected with high blood pressure throughout the Western world. Although we all need a little salt each day to balance the fluid content in our body tissue, we do not need the excessive amount that most of us add to our food daily. Salt is added to every processed food we buy; it can be canned, bottled or in a packet – surely we don't need to add more. Use herbs and spices with garlic and tomato purée instead of salt to add flavour to foods.

You will find that very few of the recipes in this book list salt among the ingredients – do try and follow them as they are given and learn to leave salt out! If you really must add salt, cut down on your normal amount.

FIBRE

Recently fibre has been well publicized and many people are aware that a diet high in fibre can actually aid slimming and prevent disorders of the bowel.

Fibre is found in breads – particularly wholemeal varieties –

and in breakfast cereals, fruit, vegetables, bran, rice and pulses. These are a valuable group of foods and many of the recipes in this book have a high fibre content.

PROTEINS

Proteins are the foods that, when digested, are used by the body to build new cells or repair worn ones. The main sources of protein are fish, meat, cheese, milk and eggs. Protein is also found in grains, nuts, seeds and pulses. Protein foods should be included in a healthy diet; try to include more vegetable proteins, such as grains, nuts, seeds, pulses or pasta, and cut down on animal proteins.

VITAMINS AND MINERALS

As long as a healthy mixed diet is followed there is no need to worry about minerals and vitamins as sufficient will be absorbed by the body from the food provided. Supplements in the form of tablets should not be necessary, but may be taken if desired.

THE MICROWAVE OVEN
AND HEALTHY EATING

The microwave oven is one of the best cooking methods available for the healthy eater:

NO-FAT COOKING

Soups may be started by softening the vegetables in a little stock with herbs instead of in fat. The onion and bacon for a quiche recipe may be started without adding fat and then drained on plenty of absorbent kitchen paper. Mince dishes may be started by microwaving the mince on its own for a few minutes and then draining off the resulting fat. When cooking meat and poultry, arrange them on a microwave roasting rack. The fat will drain from the meat and should be removed – this is ideal for all joints, chops, bacon rashers, burgers and the like. Cook fish with semi-skimmed milk and no fat in super-quick time.

LITTLE LIQUID

Fruits and vegetables may be cooked with little or no added water. Their colour and flavour therefore remain superb. They are cooked to perfection with no salt or fat. It has been proved that the loss of nutrients in microwave-cooked fruits and vegetables is less than in those foods cooked conventionally. Salt causes surface drying on vegetables and meat and it should be avoided.

HIGH-FIBRE FOODS

Wholewheat flour, vegetables, pulses, rice and pasta all microwave extremely well. Wholewheat flour adds natural colour to microwave cakes and biscuits. Use wholewheat pasta and serve with a low-fat sauce for filling lunches or suppers.

1

REHEATING

Food may be reheated quickly and efficiently with little loss of nutrients. Even pork and poultry dishes may be reheated with no fear of food poisoning as long as they are heated to a sufficient temperature. To reheat a plated meal, cover it and microwave on 100%/FULL power for about three minutes. When arranging the plate, keep denser food items, such as chops and potatoes, to the outside and leave light foods, such as peas or tomatoes, towards the centre.

SAUCES

These may be made successfully using cornflour to thicken, omitting fat, and using semi-skimmed milk or stock for healthier sauces.

THE MICROWAVE AND THE FREEZER

The microwave and freezer really are perfect partners, particularly for the healthy eater who may prefer to freeze down any extra portions of food, ready to be microwaved later – particularly useful for people who sometimes eat alone.

SPEED

Many is the time a jacket potato and a quick bowl of homemade soup, reheated in the microwave, have stopped me from reaching for the biscuit tin! I use them too when the children come home from school for a speedy nutritious snack.

CONTAINERS TO USE

Basically any container may be used as long as it has no metal content. Metal repels microwaves, or bounces them away, so food placed in metal containers won't cook. Also, metal in quantity may damage the *magnetron*, an important and expensive component of the microwave oven, so it must not be used.

There are instances when tin foil may be used in small quantities to mask certain areas of food, such as the wings of chicken, which may overcook if they are left unmasked. Clear instructions on how to do this will be given and must be adhered to, after checking with the manual supplied by your manufacturer that it is permissible to use tin foil in your particular oven.

Glass, Pyrex, pottery, china and heavy-grade plastics may all be used. There are many containers now available designed especially for microwave cooking. These are extremely useful, but use what you have in your kitchen, buying specialized containers only when necessary.

COVERING

When to cover foods – generally follow the rules relating to conventional cooking. If a moist result is required, then the food should be covered. Should a dry result, such as a cake or crumble, be preferred, then do not cover. Where possible, choose a dish with a lid when covering is called for. Failing this, the food may be placed in roasting or boil-in bags. Containers with no lid may be covered with polyethylene clingfilm, but remember to pierce the film once or lift the corner to allow steam to escape. PVC clingfilm should not be used.

STANDING TIME

The microwave cooks by weight and time, not temperature, so the more food you introduce into the oven cabinet, the longer it will take to cook. The molecules on the outside 2.5–4cm (1–1½in) of the food start to vibrate and the heat is then passed to the centre by conduction. This continues to happen after the microwaves are withdrawn, either when the microwave is switched off or when the food is removed. This continued vibration finishes the cooking process and is known as the *standing* or *equalizing* time. It is most important and should be strictly adhered to. The standing time is relevant to the density of the food, so a jacket potato will need a longer standing time than a few peas.

STIRRING AND TURNING

Stirring, or turning when stirring is not possible, such as with a cake, are important parts of microwave cookery. We stir foods to equalize the temperature throughout and prevent overcooking of the outside edge before the centre is cooked.

We turn foods to move them through the microwaves and ensure even cooking. A ¼-turn two or three times during cooking is normal. Even in those ovens which have a *turntable*, stirring and turning are still necessary.

COLOURING

There is no dry heat available in a microwave to caramelize or brown the surface of foods. However, this may easily be overcome and attractive, palatable food is produced with very little effort:

- use the grill – certain foods may be browned under the grill after microwave cooking, e.g. macaroni cheese and fish dishes. Food colours very quickly under a pre-heated grill

- use brown sugar and wholemeal flour – these will give natural colour to many foods. Paprika pepper and herbs are useful too

- brown nuts and coconut in the microwave for sprinkling on dishes – follow recipe instructions carefully

- use the browning dish, a special dish that, when pre-heated in the microwave, will become very hot across the base. It is then used as a frying pan as it will contact-brown foods such as burgers, eggs, bacon and so on. The food should be turned during cooking to brown the other side. These dishes are available in many shapes and sizes; some come with a lid and double as casserole dishes. Follow the manufacturer's instructions carefully.

CLEANING

Because the inside of the microwave never becomes really hot, cleaning is quick and simple. Wipe the interior out carefully with a dishcloth, paying particular attention to the door. Containers are easy to wash up after microwave cooking as the food doesn't 'bake' on.

SAFETY

Microwave cooking is an extremely safe method of cooking as all ovens offered for sale in the UK have to pass rigorous safety-tests. The fact that the containers and oven do not become red hot is another safety plus.

THE OUTPUT OF THE OVEN

Microwave ovens are available with different electrical outputs. Electrical output is measured in watts. Ovens available on the domestic market vary from 450W to 700W. The wattage controls the cooking time and is a very important point to take into consideration when you are selecting an oven to buy. A 700W oven will cook the food considerably quicker than an oven with an output of 450W.

COMBINATION MICROWAVE OVENS

These use traditional cooking methods combined with microwave energy. In some models both methods are used together to produce speedy 'browned' foods, while in others the microwaves and hot-air oven, or sometimes grills, are used one after the other. The recipes in this book are not designed for these ovens.

WHAT ELSE CAN THE MICROWAVE DO

As well as being able to cook food superbly, the microwave oven may be used to defrost frozen food speedily and efficiently. It will also reheat cooked foods perfectly. It may be used to dry herbs, to blanch vegetables for the freezer, to soften citrus fruits so that they yield more juice, to melt jellies, to soften chocolate, or to make jam and preserves. In fact it is an incredibly versatile piece of kitchen equipment which is also economical to run.

VARIABLE POWER

As well as DEFROST and FULL power, most ovens offer a variable-power system. Unfortunately, as these systems have not been standardized, slight variations occur from manufacturer to manufacturer. However, it is basically rather like having a thermostat on your gas or electric oven, and the different power levels are useful for different cooking operations. Use variable power in conjunction with your timer.

WHAT CAN'T BE DONE

Some things are not successful. Don't try to cook Yorkshire pudding or other batter recipes. Don't boil eggs as they may explode. Roast potatoes will not crisp and the top of a meat pie, cooked from raw, would remain soggy. However, pastry may be cooked on its own, such as when a flan is baked blind – use wholemeal flour. Deep-fat frying should not be attempted as it is impossible to control the temperature of the oil sufficiently and this could be extremely dangerous.

NOTE

The recipes given in this book were tested in a variable-power model, the Philips M710, with an output of 700W. Please note that, should your oven be less powerful, you will have to increase the stated times a little according to the output of your oven. A rough guide would be to increase cooking times by 40 seconds per minute in a 500W oven and by 20 seconds per minute in a 600W oven. You will need to decrease cooking times proportionately in an oven rated above 700W. But remember that these times are intended as a guide only, and that it is better to undercook rather than overcook – you can always pop an undercooked meal back into the oven, but an overcooked one has already been spoiled.

You will quickly get used to using the book in conjunction with your particular model.

How to be a Successful
Microwave Cook

Microwave cooking is a different, but marvellous, method of cookery. There are guidelines which should be followed so that the very best may be gained from this modern piece of kitchen equipment.

1.   Don't expect to run before you can walk! Take things slowly at first, cooking most of the meal conventionally and attempting maybe one vegetable or a sauce in the microwave so that you can give this part of the meal your undivided attention and therefore achieve perfect results.

2.   Be aware of the output (wattage) of your machine and be prepared to alter a recipe accordingly – remember that microwaves on the domestic market range between 450W and 700W, and the wattage controls the cooking time, so the timings given in a book designed for a 500W machine will have to be decreased if a 700W microwave is being used.

3.   Use a microwave cookery book carefully until you are proficient with the timings. Don't guess – bad results are disappointing and frustrating.

4.   Keep a notebook – I used to keep mine attached to the microwave and referred to it continually. Jot down your favourite recipes, hints and tips with their timings. I have discovered that families are very individual in their eating habits and, as the timing in microwave cookery is crucial, it does make sense to have the things you do often written down for you or your family to refer to constantly.

5.   Don't be afraid to seek help. Many adults see themselves as the only ones experiencing difficulties with a particular problem. I have learnt from teaching microwave cookery that it is often the basic facts that people need help with, and once a

7

question has been aired by some brave person, the point has been clarified and has helped many people.

6.   Attend demonstrations and talks, read books, and book up for microwave cookery lessons. There is plenty to learn and there is no better way of learning than actually watching an expert, as you will learn techniques, methods and many points which will help you in all aspects of microwave cookery.

7.   Use only fresh ingredients – you can't expect to get good results using inferior food.

8.   Weigh your food – even if you are not used to weighing when you cook conventionally, it is one of the most important parts of microwave cookery as the microwave cooks by weight and time, not temperature.

9.   Once you have mastered the basics of microwave cookery, use your oven at every opportunity. Experiment with converting your favourite conventional recipes. Many will microwave very well with a saving of time, energy and washing up. As a rough guide, a recipe which you enjoy cooking conventionally will take about a third to a quarter of the time when cooked in the microwave. Cakes and puddings will benefit from having a little extra liquid added when you are mixing the ingredients together, and casseroles are better with a little less liquid. Try to find a similar recipe in a microwave cookery book and use it as a guide to how much liquid to use, the power level on which to cook, when to stir, and the cooking time.

10.   Use the standing time. The standing time is suggested for a reason – the food continues to cook during this time! No harm will come to you if you eat the food before the standing time has elapsed, but it is an important part of microwave cookery, and those who believe they can slightly increase the microwave time and therefore omit the standing time are wrong. They will simply overcook the outside edge of the food while the centre may still not be cooked.

MICROWAVE KNOWLEDGE

It is often the little things which a microwave oven does so well that are not widely known. I have listed ways in which I use my microwave in the hope that my ideas, hints and tips will be useful to others. Microwave cooking is different but, once mastered, it is a quick, clean, efficient, healthy and economical method of cooking, reheating and defrosting food.

1. Covering. Remembering the recent controversy surrounding clingfilm, it is useful to have some alternative methods available – a lid to a dish is obviously ideal, but if no lid exists try:

● greaseproof paper, which may be either tucked right round and under the container to hold it in place or secured with string. If tying it with string, pierce the taut greaseproof two or three times with a skewer

● absorbent kitchen paper is useful as a covering, especially for bacon, which tends to splatter rather. It will absorb grease and so is ideal for the healthy eater

● butter muslin – used by our grandmothers daily, this old-fashioned method of covering food is ideal as it allows the steam to escape naturally and the muslin may be washed, dried and used again and again

● use plastic stacking rings and a plate – particularly useful for reheating a plated meal. Remember that the food on a plated meal should be arranged with the dense items, such as chops and potatoes, towards the outer edge and the light foods, such as peas and sprouts, towards the centre. Once covered, an average-sized plated meal will take 3–4 minutes to reheat on 100%/FULL power in a 700 W microwave oven.

2. Melting chocolate and gelatine. Use your SIMMER

SETTING, or DEFROST if SIMMER is not available, to melt these two ingredients quickly and easily. Gelatine should be sprinkled on to a little cold liquid and left to stand for 5–10 minutes before microwaving on 40%/SIMMER until melted. Chocolate is simply broken into squares, put into a Pyrex mixing bowl (so that you can see what's going on), and then microwaved – uncovered – on 40%/SIMMER. It tends to melt in its shape, so watch carefully and stir frequently.

3.   Blanch vegetables ready for freezing. The prepared vegetables should be loosely sealed in a roasting bag. Follow a microwave chart for timings and deal with only 450g (1lb) prepared vegetables at a time. Plunge the blanched vegetables immediately into a sink of ice-cold water, holding the bag down if necessary, until the vegetables are cold. Then dry the bag, label and freeze.

4.   Many foods make a loud popping sound when they are being cooked in the microwave – this is simply the fat coming to the surface. It is a common feature of microwave cooking and should be expected. It does help to stir the food when this happens, to help equalize the temperature.

5.   Use your WARM setting (20% power) for many purposes:

•   it may be used to keep a hot meal warm for up to twenty minutes. This is particularly useful for entertaining if you wish to have a drink with your guests before serving a hot meal

•   it will ripen a brie or camembert cheese

•   use it to bring red wine to room temperature – pour the wine into a jug if the bottle is too tall

•   soften butter and margarine for spreading – 225g (8oz) will take about two minutes. (Remember to remove the foil wrapper first)

•   soften the margarine and warm the sugar slightly when

making a cake – invaluable when the margarine is in the fridge and you want to make a quick cake for tea.

6. Hot spots are areas in the microwave where food tends to get hotter than in other areas. This simply means that the food placed on a 'hot spot' will cook a little quicker. As long as the food is stirred or turned during cooking so that new areas are then exposed to the 'hot spots', no real problems arise and even cooking may be easily achieved.

7. Test microwave cooking frequently. It is easy to overcook – undercooked food may be returned to the microwave for a minute or two to complete cooking, but overcooked food is spoiled.

8. Many frozen foods may be reheated from the freezer on 100%/FULL power without defrosting first. This can be very useful if guests arrive unexpectedly and the only food you have available is all frozen solid! Remember to remove any metal tag and stir frequently when stirring becomes possible. Reheat to the required temperature, keeping the dish covered.

9. Fresh herbs may be dried out between sheets of absorbent kitchen paper on 100%/FULL power. Pack and label for winter use.

10. Use your SIMMER control to reheat baby food. Stir frequently during reheating and *test often for temperature*.

11. Reheat baby's bottle. A made-up 225ml (8fl oz) bottle, taken from the refrigerator, will take roughly 45 seconds on 100%/FULL power in a 700W oven. Gently shake the bottle and *test the temperature of the milk on the inside of your wrist before giving the feed to your baby*.

12. To test if a cake is cooked. Many people experience difficulty in assessing whether a cake is cooked. The cake

should be well risen and *just* dry on the surface. As you remove it from the microwave it should release itself from the sides of the container. Another excellent test is to insert a wooden cocktail stick into the centre of the cake after its standing time. It should come out clean.

13.   Similar vegetables may be cooked together, e.g. carrots and celery, parsnips and potatoes, peas and sweetcorn. Simply prepare the weighed vegetables and arrange them in a roasting bag. Add the required liquid. Seal the bag loosely and stand it in a casserole. Microwave, turning the bag over half-way through the cooking time.

14.   Toasting nuts is very successful in the microwave. Lay the nuts out evenly on a dinner-plate and microwave until lightly golden. Rearrange the nuts several times for even toasting. Remember, they will continue to brown in their standing time, so remove them before they are too brown.

15.   Use the microwave to make jams, pickles and chutneys. Remember to choose a strong container which will cope with food reaching a very high temperature, as sugar does get very hot.

16.   Remember – the microwave cooks by weight and time, not temperature, so the more you put into the oven the longer it will take. People often don't realize that one jacket potato will take roughly 5 minutes, whilst two will take 8 minutes and three will take 11 minutes.

17.   When cooking vegetables in their skins, e.g. tomatoes, jacket potatoes and whole aubergines, remember to pierce the skins in two or three places to allow the steam to escape and to speed up the cooking process. Turning these vegetables over half-way through the cooking time is also important for even cooking.

18.   Foods such as peas, sweetcorn and carrots will cook

quicker spread out in a single layer in a fairly shallow dish rather than piled high in a smaller, tall container.

19.   Liquids expand greatly in the microwave so do use an adequate container to make sure that the liquids don't boil over when you are cooking, for example, sauces, soups, custards, pulses, rice or pasta.

20.   Invest in a wire balloon whisk (which must not be used actually in the microwave) for beating sauces, custards, scrambled eggs and so on. It will take the headache out of many recipes and enable you to produce perfect results every time.

REHEATING COOKED FOODS

The microwave oven is extremely useful for reheating cooked foods. The process is particularly speedy, and it is the best method of reheating for the healthy eater as far fewer nutrients are lost in comparison with food reheated conventionally. The starting temperature of foods will affect the reheating time, so a plated meal or a dish of cooked vegetables will take longer to reheat if it is taken from the refrigerator than it would take if reheated from room temperature.

Food should be reheated only once and must be reasonably fresh. Make sure that the food is reheated to a sufficient temperature throughout before serving. Stirring during reheating is important and will help to equalize the temperature. Turn those foods which it is impossible to stir, such as lasagne or shepherds pie. The dishes should be given a ¼-turn three or four times during reheating. Cover foods, allowing steam to escape, in most cases. Covering helps to keep the moisture in the food and speeds up the reheating process. Allow reheated foods to stand for 2–3 minutes before serving.

REHEATING CHART

Type of food	Cover	Stirring	Variable-power level	Microwave time
100g (4oz) baked beans	Yes	Yes, once	70%/ROAST	2–3 mins.
450g (16oz) baked beans	Yes	Yes, twice	70%/ROAST	7 mins.
4 cooked chops	Yes	Rearrange once	100%/FULL	3–4 mins.
Pork casserole for four	Yes	Yes, twice	100%/FULL	10–12 mins.

Type of food	Cover	Stirring	Variable-power level	Microwave time
225g (8oz) long-grain rice	Yes	–	100%/FULL	2–3 mins.
450g (1lb) cooked vegetables	Yes	Yes, once	100%/FULL	2–3 mins.
300ml (½ pint) white sauce	Yes	Yes, once	100%/FULL	2–3 mins.
1 plated meal	Yes	–	100%/FULL	3–4 mins.
6 bread rolls	Wrap in kitchen paper	Yes, rearrange once	40%/SIMMER	2–3 mins.
450g (1lb) fish	Yes	–	100%/FULL	2–3 mins.
Kedgeree for four	Yes	Yes, twice	100%/FULL	5–6 mins.
1 cup milk	–	–	100%/FULL	1½ mins.
1 mug milk	–	–	100%/FULL	2 mins.
2 chicken portions	Yes	–	100%/FULL	4 mins.
1 lasagne for four	Yes	Turn dish twice	70%/ROAST twice	10–12 mins.
1 family-size pizza	–	Turn twice	40%/ROAST	7–8 mins.
2 bowls soup	–	Yes, once	100%/FULL	5 mins.

DEFROSTING

The microwave oven really does mean that the freezer comes into its own. Foods may be rapidly and successfully defrosted from frozen. Several points must be taken into account:

- stir or turn foods during defrosting – this is extremely important if food is to be defrosted evenly

- don't try to defrost food in metal containers – it must be transferred into suitable microwave-proof dishes first

- allow a standing time between defrosting and cooking

- once it is fully defrosted, cook the food immediately.

DEFROSTING CHART

Type of food to be defrosted and weight	Variable-power level	Microwave time	Standing time
225g (8oz) butter, margarine	30%/DEFROST	2 mins.	5 mins.
225g (8oz) bacon slices	30%/DEFROST	2–3 mins.	5 mins.
Whole chicken (per 450g (1lb))	40%/SIMMER	7 mins.	20–30 mins.
4 cod steaks	40%/SIMMER	6–7 mins.	10 mins.
450g (1lb) diced steak	30%/DEFROST	6–7 mins.	10 mins.
1 large loaf bread	30%/DEFROST	6–8 mins.	10–15 mins.
100g (4oz) cream cheese	30%/DEFROST	1½ mins.	10 mins.
1 family loaf cake	30%/DEFROST	5 mins.	15 mins.
225g (8oz) rice, to heat straight from frozen	100%/FULL	4 mins.	3 mins.

Type of food to be defrosted and weight	Variable-power level	Microwave time	Standing time
4 individual suet puddings to heat straight from frozen	70%/ROAST	4–5 mins.	5 mins.
1 × 370g (14oz) packet puff pastry	30%/DEFROST	2–3 mins.	15 mins.
225g (8oz) chicken livers	30%/DEFROST	5–6 mins.	15 mins.
Quiche Lorraine for four	30%/DEFROST	5 mins.	20 mins.

RECIPES

STARTERS HOT AND COLD

The microwave comes into its own when you are preparing starters, both hot and cold. Cooking smells are kept to a minimum and the kitchen remains free from steam.

When you are entertaining, the starter may be prepared in advance and reheated as necessary when your guests arrive, a boon for the busy host or hostess.

Although designed as starters, these recipes may be served as a light lunch or supper dish. Add wholemeal bread and perhaps some feta or cottage cheese and offer fresh fruit in season.

TOFU AND PEANUT DIP

Tofu, made from the soya bean, is high in protein but low in fat and entirely free of cholesterol, making it an excellent ingredient for this tasty peanut dip. Serve with small crisp wholemeal biscuits and sticks of red pepper and celery. Very popular with children and ideal for a party.

PREPARATION TIME (after assembling ingredients): 10 minutes

MICROWAVE COOKING TIME: 2 minutes

SERVES: 8

1 medium onion, finely chopped
a few sprigs of fresh marjoram, snipped
100g (4oz) (after shelling) fresh peanuts, shelled and skins removed

100g (4oz) tofu
½ small carton (150g (5.29oz)) natural-set yoghurt
a little natural sea-salt
a few drops of tabasco or chilli sauce

1. Put the onion into a small casserole. Cover and microwave on 100%/FULL power for 2 minutes. Add the snipped marjoram. Stir and set aside until cool.

2. Put the peanuts into a food processor or liquidizer and process until chopped fairly finely.
3. Add all the remaining ingredients, including the onion and marjoram, except for the tabasco and process until smooth.
4. Add the tabasco, process again, and taste; add a little more if necessary.
5. Turn into a serving dish and refrigerate covered until ready to serve.

* To remove their skins easily, put the peanuts on a saucer and microwave on 100%/FULL power for 1 minute. Then simply rub the skins off.

CRAB PANCAKES

Use your conventional cooker in combination with your microwave and freezer to prepare the pancakes well in advance and so take the headache out of this popular starter. Wholemeal flour is high in fibre and the tasty filling uses only a little fat.

Serve one per person with a salad garnish for an impressive hot starter.

PREPARATION TIME (after assembling ingredients): 20 minutes
MICROWAVE COOKING TIME: 13½–16½ minutes
SERVES: 6

FOR THE PANCAKES
100g (4oz) wholemeal flour, plain
small pinch of salt
285ml (½ pint) semi-skimmed milk

1 large egg
1 × 5 ml spoon (1 teaspoon) olive oil
olive oil for frying

1. Put the flour and salt into a bowl. Beat together the milk, egg and 1 × 5ml spoon (1 teaspoon) oil.
2. Make a well in the flour with the back of a wooden spoon.
3. Gradually add the egg mixture to the flour, mixing with a wooden spoon, until a smooth batter results. Set aside for 1 hour before cooking.

22

4. To cook the pancakes (these must be cooked conventionally): Heat a little oil in an omelette pan, then add about 2 × 15ml spoons (2 tablespoons) batter to the hot pan, quickly tipping the pan so that the pancake forms a circle.

5. Cook until the underside browns, then flip or toss the pancake and cook the other side.

6. Turn out on to a plate and continue to cook the batter in this way until you have six pancakes.

7. Stack the pancakes between freezer paper, cool, wrap, label and freeze.

TO MAKE THE SAUCE
30g (1¼oz) wholewheat flour
30g (1¼ oz) vegetable margarine
285ml (½ pint) semi-skimmed milk
freshly ground black pepper
25g (1oz) hard Cheddar cheese, grated
1 hard-boiled egg, cooked conventionally and chopped

100g (4oz) crab meat, white and brown, fresh or frozen, but defrosted
1 × 5ml spoon (1 teaspoon) finely chopped parsley

TO GARNISH
a few sprigs of parsley
slices of lemon

1. Melt the margarine in a 1 litre (2 pint) jug on 100%/FULL power for about 1–2 minutes.

2. Stir in the flour, then gradually add the milk, mixing well. Add the parsley and the pepper.

3. Microwave on 100%/FULL power for about 4 minutes, or until the sauce rises well in the jug. Beat well with a balloon whisk after 2 minutes and again at the end of the cooking time. Beat in the grated cheese.

4. Shred the crab and fold into the sauce with the hard-boiled egg.

To complete the dish

5. Microwave the frozen pancakes for 5–7 minutes on DE-FROST. Let stand for 5 minutes. They will be almost thawed and easy to handle.

6. Divide the filling between the pancakes, spreading it over evenly with a knife.

7. Roll the pancakes up and arrange in a suitable dish. Cover with clingfilm and pierce.
8. Microwave on 100%/FULL power for about 3½ minutes to reheat.
9. Serve immediately, garnished with the lemon and parsley.

SPINACH AND TUNA MOULD

Prepared well in advance, this colourful starter is served cold. Salmon could be used instead of the tuna for a slightly richer taste. Ideal for a summer's evening dinner party. Spinach, an excellent source of vitamins A and C, is combined with high-protein foods in this attractive dish.

PREPARATION TIME (after assembling ingredients):
    20 minutes
MICROWAVE COOKING TIME: 23–8 minutes
SERVES: 4–6

450g (1lb) fresh spinach
1 198g (7oz) can tuna fish in oil, drained
100g (4oz) medium-fat cream cheese or cottage cheese
vegetable oil for greasing

175ml (4fl oz) semi-skimmed milk
4 eggs, size 2
1 clove garlic, chopped
freshly ground black pepper
tomato sauce (see p. 45)

To serve warm

1. Trim the stalks from the spinach and wash it well in two or three changes of cold water.
2. Put the spinach into a roasting bag, stand the bag in a bowl, and seal the opening loosely with an elastic band.
3. Microwave on 100%/FULL power for 6–8 minutes, turning the bag over once after 3 minutes. Set aside for 5 minutes.
4. Put the tuna and cream cheese or cottage cheese into the food processor or liquidizer. Add 1 egg and process until puréed. Turn into a lightly oiled 1 litre (2 pint) fluted mould.
5. Wash out the liquidizer or food processor, then put the *drained* spinach into it.

6. Add the milk with the remaining eggs and the garlic and black pepper. Process to combine.
7. Turn on to the tuna and cheese mixture. Cover with clingfilm and microwave on 50%/MEDIUM for 17–20 minutes, or until firm to the touch. Give the dish a ¼-turn after 10 minutes.
8. Leave to cool for about 30 minutes, then ease round the edge with your finger. Turn out and serve with the Tomato Sauce (see p. 45), but do not add the peanut butter to the sauce.

* The cooked spinach must be drained well in a sieve.

* Watch the cooking time on 50%/MEDIUM closely. Different microwaves will take different times to set this dish.

HADDOCK MOUSSE

It is easy to dissolve gelatine if you use the SIMMER control on your microwave. This light fish mousse may be prepared well in advance. When ready to serve, turn out and garnish with crimped cucumber – super on a buffet table! Remember that the haddock will continue to cook during the standing time. This light mousse is low in fat and high in protein.

PREPARATION TIME (after assembling ingredients):
    25 minutes
MICROWAVE COOKING TIME: 9–12 minutes
SERVES: 4

225g (8oz) smoked haddock
285ml (½ pint) semi-skimmed milk
freshly ground black pepper
15g (½oz) polyunsaturated margarine
2 × 15ml spoons (2 tablespoons) cornflour, level
50g (2oz) Gouda cheese, grated

1 × 15ml spoon (1 tablespoon) powdered gelatine
3 × 15ml spoons (3 tablespoons) fish stock or water
2 egg whites

TO GARNISH
crimped cucumber

1. Arrange the haddock on a shallow dish, masking the thin tails with a little tin foil.

2. Pour over 2 × 15ml spoons (2 tablespoons) of the milk. Season with black pepper. Dot with the margarine.

3. Cover with clingfilm and pierce once, or use a lid. Microwave on 100%/FULL power for 4–5 minutes. Set aside, covered, until cold.

4. Make the sauce: Use a little of the remaining milk to cream the cornflour to a smooth paste in a 1.7 litre (3 pint) bowl.

5. Put the remaining milk into a jug and microwave on 100%/FULL power for 2 minutes.

6. Pour the heated milk on to the creamed cornflour, stirring continuously, then microwave on 100%/FULL power, uncovered, for 1–2 minutes, or until boiling and thickened. Stir every minute.

7. Stir the grated cheese into the sauce with some black pepper. Stir until the cheese has melted. Set aside.

8. Put the liquor from the fish into a small bowl with the fish stock or water. Sprinkle on the gelatine. Allow to stand for 5 minutes, then microwave on 40%/SIMMER for 2–3 minutes. Stir to ensure that the gelatine has dissolved.

9. Fold the dissolved gelatine into the cheese sauce. Allow to cool completely, then fold in the flaked fish, discarding the skin.

10. Whisk the egg whites and fold in lightly.

11. Pour into a 1 litre (2 pint) wetted mould and refrigerate until set firm.

12. Turn out and serve garnished with crimped cucumber.

* To turn out: Fill the sink with very hot water. Hold the mould in this water, almost up to the top. Count to eight. Remove the mould from the water and turn out on to a serving dish.

SPINACH WITH PRAWNS

A tasty light starter which is eye-appealing and good to eat. The recipe is low in fat and easy to prepare.

PREPARATION TIME (after assembling ingredients):
5 minutes

MICROWAVE COOKING TIME: 18–19 minutes
SERVES: 4

2 × 227g (8 oz) blocks frozen
  chopped spinach
100g (4oz) Edam cheese,
  grated
2 cloves garlic, chopped
1 × 15ml (1 tablespoon)
  chopped chives

freshly ground black pepper
227g (8oz) peeled prawns,
  defrosted if frozen

TO SERVE
toasted wholemeal bread

1. Cut open the packets of spinach so that it will be easy to squeeze out the spinach when it is cooked. Lay the packets side by side on two sheets of absorbent kitchen paper in a shallow dish.
2. Microwave on 100%/FULL power for 11 minutes, turning each packet over once half-way through.
3. Drain the spinach well by putting it into a sieve and pressing the water out with a wooden spoon.
4. Turn the drained spinach into a bowl. Add the cheese, garlic, chives and pepper. Mix to combine. Turn into a serving dish.
5. Top with the prawns – drain on kitchen paper if frozen.
6. Cover with clingfilm and pierce.
7. Microwave on 40%/SIMMER for 7–8 minutes, giving the dish a ¼-turn twice during this time.
8. Serve immediately with toasted wholemeal bread.

TUNA PÂTÉ

The cheese, vegetables and tuna fish combine to make a delicious pâté which may be used as a sandwich filling for packed lunches or served with a salad as a refreshing starter – choose curly endive or some crisp iceberg lettuce leaves with crimped cucumber and sprigs of watercress. A high-protein, low-fat pâté.

PREPARATION TIME (after assembling ingredients):
   12 minutes

MICROWAVE COOKING TIME: 3 minutes
SERVES: 4

1 small onion, chopped
1 × 15ml spoon (1 tablespoon)
corn oil
1 × 5ml spoon (1 teaspoon)
dried parsley
75g (3oz) button mushrooms,
chopped
1 × 198g (7oz) can tuna fish in
oil, drained
100g (4oz) skimmed-milk soft
cheese

1 × 5ml spoon (1 teaspoon)
tomato purée
1 × 5ml spoon (1 teaspoon)
whole-grain mustard
2 × 5ml spoons (2 teaspoons)
lemon juice
freshly ground black pepper

TO SERVE
wholemeal toast and salad
garnish

1. Put the onion and oil into a medium-sized bowl and micro-
    wave, uncovered, on 100%/FULL power for 2 minutes,
    stirring after 1 minute.
2. Stir in the parsley and mushrooms and microwave on
    100%/FULL power for 1 minute. Set aside to cool.
3. Transfer to a liquidizer or food processor. Flake in the
    drained tuna, and add the skimmed-milk soft cheese,
    tomato purée, mustard, lemon juice and pepper.
4. Process or liquidize to combine.
5. Turn into a suitable container. Cover and chill until ready
    to serve.

BUTTERBEAN SOUP

The microwave cooks pulses beautifully. Here butterbeans add
fibre and protein to a vegetable soup.

Almost a meal in itself, this colourful soup is popular with
young and old alike.

PREPARATION TIME (after assembling ingredients):
15 minutes
MICROWAVE COOKING TIME: 58–9 minutes
SERVES: 4

100g (4oz) dried butterbeans
  soaked overnight
1 red pepper, deseeded and
  roughly chopped
1 medium onion, peeled and
  chopped
100g (4oz) fresh cauliflower
  florets
1 medium leek or 1 medium
  courgette, sliced

825ml (1½ pint) well-flavoured
  stock, boiling
1 × 15ml spoon (1 tablespoon)
  cornflour

TO SERVE
plenty of freshly chopped
  parsley

1. Drain the butterbeans and rinse well. Put the beans into a 3 litre (6 pint) casserole and cover with boiling water.
2. Cover with a lid and microwave on 100%/FULL power for 35 minutes. Set aside, covered, for 10 minutes.
3. Drain the beans and return to the casserole.
4. Add the red pepper, onion and cauliflower, and the leek or courgette.
5. Add the stock and stir. Cover with a lid and microwave on 100%/FULL power for 20 minutes, stirring and re-covering after 10 minutes.
6. Allow to stand for 5 minutes.
7. Cream the cornflour to a smooth paste with a little water and stir into the soup.
8. Microwave, uncovered, for 3–4 minutes, stirring every minute, or until boiling and thickened slightly. Serve sprinkled with freshly chopped parsley.

STUFFED TOMATOES

When tomatoes are plentiful this starter may be made from store cupboard ingredients. Sometimes I serve these as a vegetable with a fish dish – they add colour to the plate and are lovely and moist to eat. A high-fibre starter, ideal for vegetarians.

PREPARATION TIME (after assembling ingredients):
  12 minutes

MICROWAVE COOKING TIME: 20–22 minutes
SERVES: 4

50g (2oz) brown rice
1 clove garlic, crushed
   (optional)
2 spring onions, chopped
315ml (11fl oz) light stock,
   chicken or vegetable,
   boiling
4 large ripe tomatoes, total
   weight 556g (1¼lb)
15ml (1 tablespoon) chopped
   walnuts or chopped brazil
   nuts

25g (1oz) raisins
2 × 5ml spoons (2 teaspoons)
   tomato purée
freshly ground black pepper
½ × 5ml spoon (½ teaspoon)
   ground allspice

TO SERVE
cottage cheese and chives or a
   yoghurt and chive dressing

1. Put the rice into a 1.7 litre (3 pint) bowl with the garlic, if
   used, and the spring onions. Pour on the boiling stock.
2. Cover with a lid and microwave on 100%/FULL power for 15
   minutes. Set aside for 12 minutes, *without* removing the lid.
3. Prepare the tomatoes. Cut the round end off (this will then
   be the lid) and scoop out the core and seeds but be careful not
   to remove the flesh.
4. Fork up the rice after its standing time and add the walnuts
   or brazils, raisins and tomato purée with the pepper and
   allspice. Mix well.
5. Fill the tomatoes with the prepared stuffing. Top with the
   reserved lids and stand on a serving dish.
6. Microwave on 50%/MEDIUM for 5–7 minutes, turning each
   tomato once after 1 minute.
7. Allow to stand for 5 minutes, then serve hot with a spoonful
   of cottage cheese and chives on each plate.

* The 'round' end of a tomato is the end opposite the stalk.

WARMING VEGETABLE SOUP

Naturally thickened with root vegetables, this is an easy soup to
make. The ingredients are all readily available and the flavour
is light. A satisfying soup that is high in fibre and has only a
small amount of fat added in the milk.

PREPARATION TIME (after assembling ingredients):
15 minutes

MICROWAVE COOKING TIME: 32 minutes

SERVES: 4

225g (8oz) potatoes, peeled and diced
100g (4oz) carrots, peeled and diced
225g (8oz) parsnips, peeled and diced
1 medium leek, washed and sliced
550ml (1 pint) well-flavoured chicken stock, hot

3 sprigs marjoram, tied together
freshly ground black pepper
285ml (½ pint) semi-skimmed milk, cold

TO GARNISH
freshly chopped parsley

1. Put the potato, carrot, parsnip and leek into a 2.3 litre (4 pint) bowl with the hot stock and the marjoram.
2. Cover with a lid and microwave on 100%/FULL power for 20 minutes, stirring and re-covering after 8 minutes.
3. Stir and set aside, covered, for 15 minutes. Remove the marjoram and discard.
4. Using a draining spoon, transfer the cooked vegetables to the food processor or liquidizer. Add just enough of the hot liquid for the machine to run smoothly and then process the ingredients until smooth.
5. Return to the large bowl, blending with a spoon. Season with the pepper, then stir in the milk.
6. Reheat, covered, for 12 minutes on 40%/SIMMER, stirring twice during reheating.
7. Serve immediately sprinkled with freshly chopped parsley.

GARLIC-STUFFED MUSHROOMS

Always a firm favourite. This delicious starter microwaves extremely well and uses very little fat in its preparation. Mushrooms are an excellent source of B vitamins.

31

PREPARATION TIME (after assembling ingredients):
   10 minutes
MICROWAVE COOKING TIME: 6–7 minutes
SERVES: 4

4 large flat mushrooms (now
   available in most
   supermarkets)
2 × 15ml spoons (2
   tablespoons) rapeseed oil
1 medium onion, finely
   chopped
1 stick celery, finely chopped
50g (2oz) fresh brown
   breadcrumbs

1 clove garlic, chopped
2 × 15ml spoons (2
   tablespoons) Parmesan
   cheese

TO SERVE
extra Parmesan cheese, sprigs
   of parsley, and a Webbs
   Wonder lettuce

1. Remove the stalks from the mushrooms by carefully rocking them backwards and forwards. Chop the stalks.
2. Brush the mushrooms, inside and out, with the oil. Stand on a serving dish – a dinner-plate is ideal.
3. Put the onion and celery into a medium bowl. Cover and microwave on 100%/FULL power for 2 minutes. Stir in the breadcrumbs, garlic and Parmesan cheese with the chopped stalks. Mix well, adding any remaining oil to bind the ingredients.
4. Divide the filling evenly between the mushrooms.
5. Microwave, uncovered, on 100%/FULL power for 4–5 minutes. Serve immediately sprinkled with a little extra grated Parmesan and a sprig of parsley on a Webbs lettuce garnish.

WATERCRESS SOUP

The combination of potato and onion with the watercress gives this soup a subtle flavour and an attractive colour. I serve it as a starter for a winter dinner party, as prepared beforehand it takes only 8–10 minutes to reheat in a large container and is ideal for adult guests.

Watercress contains iron and also vitamins A and C.

PREPARATION TIME (after assembling ingredients):
10 minutes
MICROWAVE COOKING TIME: 29 minutes
SERVES: 4

1 medium onion, peeled and
chopped
225g (8oz) potato, peeled and
diced
100g (4oz) watercress, thick
stalks discarded
550ml (1 pint) well-flavoured
chicken or meat stock, cold

825ml (½ pint) semi-skimmed
milk

TO GARNISH
1 small onion, peeled and
ringed, reserved watercress
sprigs

1. Put the onion and potato into a 2.3 litre (4 pint) bowl and cover with a lid.
2. Microwave on 100%/FULL for 5 minutes, stirring and re-covering after 3 minutes.
3. Reserve 4 tiny sprigs of watercress for garnish and chop the remainder. Add to the soup with the stock and milk and stir well.
4. Cover and microwave on 100%/FULL power for 12 minutes. Stir after 5 minutes. Allow to stand, covered, for 5 minutes, then using a slotted spoon transfer vegetables and watercress to a food processor or liquidizer.
5. Add about 1 cupful of the liquid and process or liquidize until smooth.
6. Return contents of liquidizer or food processor to the large bowl, stirring to mix the ingredients thoroughly.
7. Cover and return to the microwave for 10 minutes on 40%/SIMMER, stirring after 3 minutes and again at end of the cooking time.
8. Set aside, covered, while preparing the garnish.
9. Simply put the prepared onion rings into an 825ml (1½ pint) bowl. Cover and microwave on 100%/FULL power for 2 minutes. Set aside for 2 minutes.
10. Pour the soup into a warmed tureen and add the onion rings.

11. Float the reserved sprigs of watercress on the surface and serve immediately with French bread.

* This soup is also delicious chilled.

ONION SOUP

Using the microwave means the onions can be sweated in very little oil, resulting in a healthy soup that's bursting with taste. The wholemeal bread and half-fat Cheddar cheese topping makes a welcome alternative to the traditional Gruyère.

PREPARATION TIME (after assembling ingredients):
20 minutes
MICROWAVE COOKING TIME:
26 minutes plus grilling time
SERVES: 4

2 × 15ml spoons (2 tablespoons) olive oil
675g (1½lb) onions, peeled and thinly sliced
1 clove garlic, crushed
1 × 5ml (1 level teaspoon) finely chopped parsley
825ml (1½ pint) well-flavoured beef stock, cold
freshly ground black pepper

FOR THE TOPPING
8 thick slices, cut from a wholemeal French stick
50g (2oz) half-fat Cheddar cheese crumbled

TO SERVE
finely chopped fresh parsley (optional)

1. Put the olive oil into a 2.3 litre (4 pint) bowl and microwave for 1 minute on 100%/FULL power.
2. Stir in the onion and garlic.
3. Cover and microwave on 100%/FULL power for 10 minutes, stirring and re-covering after 5 minutes.
4. Stir in the parsley and the stock. Season with pepper.
5. Cover and microwave on 100%/FULL power for 15 minutes, stirring and re-covering after 6 minutes.
6. Allow to stand, covered, inside or outside the microwave for 5 minutes while preparing the topping.

7. Arrange the bread, in a single layer, on a grill-proof dish or plate.
8. Pop the bread under a pre-heated grill until it is just starting to colour.
9. Using oven gloves, remove and top the bread evenly with the grated cheese. Grill until golden.
10. I find it easiest to serve the soup in individual bowls, dividing the topping between them, by simply sliding the bread slices on to the hot soup using a knife while holding the plate or dish with oven gloves.
11. Sprinkle with finely chopped fresh parsley if liked.

* There will be very few lingering smells in the kitchen after you have made this pungent soup!

HOT GRAPEFRUIT

A very simple but delicious way to serve grapefruit. Popular at any time of year and a useful source of vitamin C.

PREPARATION TIME (after assembling ingredients):
5–10 minutes
MICROWAVE COOKING TIME: 2–3 minutes
SERVES: 4

2 medium grapefruits   a little ground cinnamon
4 × 5ml spoons (4 teaspoons)
  clear honey

1. Halve each grapefruit and loosen segments using a grapefruit knife. Arrange in shallow sundae dishes.
2. Dribble 1 × 5ml spoon (1 teaspoon) of honey on each grapefruit half.
3. Sprinkle each half with a little cinnamon.

* When you are using citrus fruits in any recipe, they will be much easier to juice, and will indeed yield more juice, if microwaved first. Simply put the fruits on to a plate and microwave, uncovered, on 100%/FULL power until slightly warm: for example, 4 medium oranges will take about 1½ minutes.

4. Microwave all 4 together, uncovered, for 2–3 minutes on 100%/FULL power, rearranging the grapefruit halves once during this time.
5. Serve immediately.

MUSHROOM PÂTÉ

The combination of mushrooms and quark gives a superbly rich taste but provides an easily digested pâté which is delicious served with pieces of raw young vegetables, such as celery, cauliflower or red pepper, and some wholemeal toast. Butter is used here for its excellent flavour.

PREPARATION TIME (after assembling ingredients):
   10 minutes
MICROWAVE COOKING TIME: 4½ minutes
SERVES: 6

25g (1oz) butter
150g (6oz) flat mushrooms, chopped
1 medium onion, chopped
1 clove garlic, chopped
a handful of fresh parsley sprigs

2 × 5ml spoons (2 teaspoons) lemon juice
200g (7oz) quark (skimmed milk, low-fat soft cheese)

1. Put the butter into a 1.7 litre (3 pint) casserole and micro-wave on 100%/FULL power for 30 seconds, or until melted.
2. Stir in the prepared mushrooms, onion and garlic.
3. Cover and microwave on 100%/FULL power for 4 minutes, stirring and re-covering after 2 minutes.
4. Stir in the parsley. Re-cover and set aside to cool.
5. When the mixture is cool, transfer to a liquidizer or food processor. Add the lemon juice and quark. Process until smooth.
6. Turn into a serving dish. Level the top and cover. Chill for at least an hour before serving.

36

Avocado Pâté

Spread this light pâté on to toast or biscuits and serve with a selection of olives or some crisp celery. Ideal for vegetarians. Avocados are rich in vitamins A, B, C, D and E and in calcium.

PREPARATION TIME (after assembling ingredients):
   15 minutes
MICROWAVE COOKING TIME: 2 minutes
SERVES: 4

1 stick celery, chopped
1 small onion, chopped
1 × 15ml spoon (1 tablespoon)
   olive oil
½ × 5ml spoon (½ teaspoon)
   dried basil
1 ripe avocado

3 × 15ml spoons (3
   tablespoons) ground
   almonds
freshly ground black pepper
1 × 5ml spoon (1 teaspoon)
   lemon juice

1. Put the celery, onion and oil into a medium bowl.
2. Cover and microwave on 100%/FULL power for 2 minutes.
3. Stir in the basil, cover and set aside to cool.
4. Put the cooled celery and onion mixture into a liquidizer or food processor. Process to chop very finely.
5. Peel and chop the avocado and add the flesh to the processor or liquidizer with the ground almonds, lemon juice and pepper.
6. Process to combine.
7. Turn into a dish. Cover and chill until ready to serve.

*   If you reserve the stone from the avocado and put it in the middle of the pâté while it is in the fridge, it will prevent discoloration.

Dressed Vegetables with Feta Cheese

Vegetables cooked in the microwave are excellent, full of flavour and colour, with very little loss of food value. This starter with a Greek touch is super for dinner parties. Serve with warm wholemeal bread. A high-fibre dish with little added fat.

PREPARATION TIME (after assembling ingredients):
15 minutes
MICROWAVE COOKING TIME: 6–8 minutes
SERVES: 4

1 medium red pepper, cut into
  strips
1 medium green pepper, cut
  into strips
100g (4oz) tiny button
  mushrooms, stalks removed
2 carrots, peeled and cut into
  matchsticks
1 courgette, sliced
1 stick celery, cut into
  matchsticks
2 × 15ml spoons (2
  tablespoons) white wine

FOR THE DRESSING
3 × 15ml spoon (3 tablespoons)
  walnut oil
1 × 15ml spoon (1 tablespoon)
  white wine vinegar
5ml (1 teaspoon) lemon juice
15ml (1 tablespoon) freshly
  chopped parsley
freshly ground black pepper

TO SERVE
50g (2oz) feta cheese

1. Put all the prepared vegetables into a roasting bag. Add the
    wine. Stand the bag in a casserole dish and fold the opening
    under or seal it loosely with an elastic band.
2. Microwave on 100%/FULL power for 6–8 minutes, turning
    the bag over once half-way through.
3. Set aside for 5 minutes.
4. To make the dressing: Combine the oil, vinegar, lemon
    juice, parsley and ground black pepper, and whisk with a
    fork.
5. Turn the vegetables, with their liquid, into a serving dish.
6. Pour over the dressing and toss to coat. Cover, and set aside
    to cool.
7. Serve cold, on individual side-plates, sprinkled with the
    crumbled feta cheese.

*   As an alternative: Just before serving add 1 pear *or* apple cored and
    sliced, but not peeled; *or* 1 orange, segmented, discarding the peel,
    pith and pips; *or* ½ melon, balled or diced.

CHICKEN LIVER PÂTÉ

The flavour will improve if this pâté is made a day or two in advance and the ramekins are kept covered in the refrigerator. Store them below the middle shelf where the fridge is not quite so cold. Liver and cottage cheese are protein foods. Liver contains vitamins A and B complex and iron in appreciable amounts.

PREPARATION TIME (after assembling ingredients):
   15 minutes
MICROWAVE COOKING TIME: 5–6 minutes
SERVES: 4

225g (8oz) chicken livers
2 × 15ml spoons (2 tablespoons) olive oil
1 clove garlic, crushed
freshly ground black pepper
113g (4 oz) cottage cheese

1 × 5ml spoon (1 teaspoon) tomato purée

TO SERVE
1 × 5ml spoon (1 teaspoon) fresh parsley sprigs
wholemeal toast

1. Pick over the chicken livers and discard any membranes.
2. Put the oil into a 1.7 litre (3 pint) bowl and microwave for 1 minute on 100%/FULL power.
3. Stir in the garlic and the chicken livers. Season lightly with pepper.
4. Cover and microwave on 70%/ROAST for 4–5 minutes, stirring and re-covering after 1 minute. Stir and set aside until cold.
5. Transfer to a liquidizer or food processor and add the tomato purée and the cottage cheese. Process or liquidize until smooth.
6. Divide between four ramekins. Level the tops. Cover with clingfilm and refrigerate.
7. Serve garnished with the parsley sprigs, with some warm wholemeal toast.

* To defrost 225g (8oz) frozen chicken livers will take about 6 minutes using the DEFROST control. Allow to stand for 15 minutes after defrosting and before making the pâté.

CHINESE STARTER

Crisp vegetables with a nut and breadcrumb topping make a fibre-full starter. Lime juice and ginger give an oriental flavour while the microwave ensures that this starter is cooked to perfection.

PREPARATION TIME (after assembling ingredients):
20 minutes

MICROWAVE COOKING TIME: 9–11 minutes

SERVES: 4

2 × 15ml spoons (2 tablespoons) grapeseed oil
1 × 15ml spoon (1 tablespoon) light soya sauce
1 × 15ml spoon (1 tablespoon) chopped fresh ginger
rind and juice of 1 lime
1 medium red pepper, deseeded and cut into strips
1 medium green pepper, deseeded and cut into strips
2 large flat mushrooms, wiped and sliced

6 spring onions, cut in half lengthways
2 sticks celery, cut into matchsticks
1 leek sliced

FOR THE TOPPING
25g (1oz) blanched almonds, chopped
25g (1oz) brown breadcrumbs

1.   Prepare the topping: Put 2 × 5ml spoons (2 teaspoons) of the oil into a medium-sized bowl. Stir in the nuts and breadcrumbs to coat with oil.
2.   Microwave on 100%/FULL power for 3–5 minutes, stirring every minute, or until lightly coloured. Set aside, stirring occasionally while vegetables are cooking.
3.   Put remaining oil into a large, fairly shallow dish, the sort you might serve a spaghetti dish in.
4.   Microwave on 100%/FULL power for 1 minute.
5.   Add all the prepared vegetables with the soya sauce and ginger and the lime juice. Toss well.
6.   Cover and microwave on 100%/FULL power for 5 minutes, stirring and re-covering after 3 minutes.

*   This also makes an attractive vegetable dish for a buffet party. Add the crispy topping just before serving.

7. Stir and serve on four side-plates, sprinkled with the crispy topping.

CHICK PEA PÂTÉ

An inexpensive and nutritious starter. Chick pea pâté, or humous, is so popular that I always keep some chick peas in the store-cupboard. Serve humous with tuna or chicken liver pâté so that guests can have a little of each as their starter. Chick peas are high in fibre and also provide protein.

PREPARATION TIME (after assembling ingredients):
   10 minutes
MICROWAVE COOKING TIME: 43 minutes
SERVES: 4

100g (4oz) (weighed dry) chick peas, soaked and then drained
1 small onion, finely chopped
3 × 15ml spoons (3 tablespoons) olive oil
1 stick celery, finely chopped

1 × 15ml spoon (1 tablespoon) lemon juice
a little sea-salt

TO SERVE
warm wholemeal bread

1. Put the chick peas into a 2.3 litre (4 pint) casserole and cover with 1.7 litres (3 pints) boiling water from the kettle.
2. Cover with a lid and microwave on 100%/FULL power for 40 minutes. Allow to stand until cool.
3. Put the onion, oil and celery into a medium bowl. Cover and microwave on 100%/FULL power for 3 minutes. Stir and set aside to cool.
5. Using a slotted spoon, lift the chick peas into a food processor bowl or liquidizer. Retain the liquid. Add the celery and onion mixture with the lemon juice and the salt. Liquidize or process to combine. Add 55ml (2fl oz) of the reserved cooking liquid and process until smooth.
6. Turn into a suitable serving dish. Cover and chill until ready to serve.

7.   I garnish this dish with a single slice of fresh lemon.

*   The chick peas should be soaked in plenty of cold water for at least 4 hours, then rinsed well, before you make the pâté.

MINESTRONE SOUP

Made the microwave way, this soup is full of flavour but low on fat. A satisfying Italian way to start any meal.

> PREPARATION TIME (after assembling ingredients):
>   15 minutes
> MICROWAVE COOKING TIME: 23 minutes
> SERVES: 4

1 × 15ml (1 tablespoon) corn oil
1 onion, peeled and chopped
1–2 cloves garlic, crushed
1 carrot, peeled and cut into matchsticks
1 stick celery, cut into matchsticks
1 medium courgette, sliced
50g (2oz) short-cut macaroni
2 × 5ml spoons (2 teaspoons) dried oregano or parsley
700ml (1¼ pint) well-flavoured chicken stock, boiling

4 tomatoes, skinned and chopped
3 × 15ml spoons (3 tablespoons) frozen peas
salt and freshly ground black pepper
2 × 15ml spoons (2 tablespoons) tomato purée

TO SERVE
grated Parmesan cheese

1.   Put the oil into a 2.3 litre (4 pint) bowl and microwave, uncovered, for 1 minute on 100%/FULL power.
2.   Stir in the onion, garlic, carrot, celery and courgette.
3.   Cover with a lid and microwave on 100%/FULL power for 5 minutes.
4.   Stir in the macaroni, with the oregano or parsley, the boiling stock and the tomatoes, and season.
5.   Cover and microwave on 100%/FULL power for 15 minutes, stirring and re-covering after 7 minutes.
6.   Stir in the peas and tomato purée. Cover and microwave on 100%/FULL power for 2 minutes.

7. Set aside, covered, for 5 minutes.
8. Serve piping hot and hand a bowl of grated Parmesan cheese round separately.

* To reheat 1 bowl of soup, uncovered, will take about 3 minutes on 100%/FULL power. Two will take about 5 minutes. In both cases stand the bowl(s) on tea-plates for easier handling during reheating and stir before serving.

CHICKEN STOCK

Stock cubes, although useful store-cupboard ingredients, often contain concentrations of salt and monosodium glutamate or flavour-enhancer. Artificial colouring is also often added. Either buy low-salt stock cubes from a reputable health food store or, better still, make your own in the microwave, as the kitchen will remain free of steam and the lingering smell, which you may not like, will be cut down.

This no-salt stock will freeze well – freeze it down in ice cube trays and when frozen bag it up and label. This is an easy way to have small quantities of stock readily available.

This recipe makes about 1.4 litres (2½ pints)

PREPARATION TIME (after assembling ingredients):
    10 minutes
MICROWAVE COOKING TIME: about 2 hours

1 chicken carcass cooked or raw with any extra skin or bones and any jelly left over
225g (8oz) carrots, peeled and roughly chopped
225g (8oz) celery, roughly chopped

a bunch of fresh herbs, tied securely, or 1 × 5ml spoon (1 teaspoon) dried herbs
6 black peppercorns

1. Put the carcass, with any extra skin and bones and any jelly if available, into a 2.3–2.8 litre (4–5 pint) bowl.
2. Add the vegetables, herbs and peppercorns. Pour on 1.7 litres (3 pints) cold water.

3. Cover with a lid and microwave on 100%/FULL power for 25–30 minutes or until boiling.
4. Continue to microwave on DEFROST for 1½ hours.
5. Remove the scum. Allow the stock to cool, strain, and then refrigerate, and when it is cold remove any fat.

* *Brown stock* is made in the same way using about a kilo (2½lbs) beef bones available from the butcher.

* *Fish stock* is quicker to make. Ask the fishmonger to sell you about 175g (1½lb) fish heads and tails. Put them into a large bowl with 225g (8oz) mixed root vegetables, roughly chopped. Add 825ml (1½ pints) cold water, a handful of fresh herbs and 6 peppercorns. Cover with a lid and microwave on 100%/FULL power for about 12 minutes or until boiling. Remove the scum. Cover and microwave on DEFROST for 30 minutes. Allow to cool slightly, remove the scum again if necessary, then strain and cool until required.

This recipe makes about 825ml (1½ pints).

SPAGHETTI WITH TOMATO AND PEANUT SAUCE

Make this in late summer, when tomatoes are cheap and bursting with flavour. The microwave cooks spaghetti beautifully without it boiling over and there are no sticky pans to wash up afterwards. Tomatoes are rich in vitamin A and the pasta provides carbohydrate and fibre.

PREPARATION TIME (after assembling ingredients):
    25 minutes
MICROWAVE COOKING TIME: 28–30 minutes
SERVES: 4

225g (8oz) quick-cooking spaghetti
1 × 5 ml spoon (1 teaspoon) olive oil

FOR THE SAUCE
900g (2lb) ripe tomatoes, peeled and chopped
1 × 15ml spoon (1 tablespoon) olive oil
1 small onion, peeled and chopped

1 × 5ml spoon (1 teaspoon) dried mixed herbs
1 clove garlic, crushed
freshly ground black pepper
1 × 15ml spoon (1 tablespoon) smooth peanut butter

TO GARNISH
some freshly snipped basil

1. Prepare the tomatoes: Put the tomatoes into a large bowl and cover with boiling water, from the kettle. As soon as the skins 'split', take them out of the water and peel them, using a knife and fork for easy handling. Chop the skinned tomatoes and discard any hard bits of core.
2. Make the sauce: Put the olive oil, together with the onion, into a 2.3 litre (4 pint) casserole and microwave, uncovered, on 100%/FULL power for 2 minutes.
3. Stir in the tomatoes, mixed herbs and garlic, and season with some black pepper.
4. Microwave, uncovered, on 100%/FULL power for 10 minutes. Stir.
5. Continue to microwave, uncovered, on 100%/FULL power for 8 minutes to reduce slightly. Stir in the peanut butter. Set aside.
6. Cook the spaghetti: Pour a kettle of boiling water into a 2.3 litre (4 pint) bowl. Hold the spaghetti in the water until it softens sufficiently to bend, then gently push it into the water, until it is completely immersed. Add the teaspoon of oil.
7. Cover and microwave on 100%/FULL power for 6–8 minutes, stirring once after 3 minutes with the handle of a wooden spoon – this will stop the spaghetti sticking together.
8. Allow to stand, covered, for 2 minutes, drain and rinse well with boiling water, then drain again and transfer to a serving dish.
9. Pop the tomato sauce back into the microwave for 2 minutes on 100%/FULL power, to reheat, then stir and pour over the cooked spaghetti.
10. Sprinkle with a little chopped fresh basil before serving.

BAKED EGGS WITH CRAB

Eggs, although a high-cholesterol food, are high in protein and low in calories. Eggs should be eaten only two or three times a

45

week, so I have included this baked-egg recipe that is quick and easy to prepare in the microwave.

PREPARATION TIME (after assembling ingredients):
    2 minutes
MICROWAVE COOKING TIME: 4–6 minutes
SERVES: 4

4 eggs, size 2
freshly ground black pepper

170g (6oz) cooked crab meat,
    defrosted if frozen

1. Put 1 × 15ml spoon (1 tablespoon) cold water into each of four individual ramekins.
2. Arrange them in ring fashion in the microwave.
3. Microwave on 100%/FULL power until the water boils.
4. Carefully crack 1 egg into each dish. Prick each yolk with a cocktail stick.
5. Season with a little black pepper.
6. Cover each dish with clingfilm and pierce once.
7. Microwave on 40%/SIMMER for 4–6 minutes, or until the whites are just set. Turn the dishes once during the cooking time.
8. Allow to stand for 2–3 minutes, then drain off the water. Divide the crab meat evenly between the ramekins, arranging it so that the yolk is still visible.
9. Serve immediately with toasted wholemeal bread.

NEW POTATOES AND CELERY WITH COTTAGE CHEESE DIP

Potatoes are known as carbohydrate, or energy-giving, foods. They also contain protein, vitamins and minerals. Cooked without fat they contain only 23 calories per ounce. Serve them with this delicious dip as a starter – very popular with children.

PREPARATION TIME (after assembling ingredients):
    10 minutes

MICROWAVE COOKING TIME: 11–12 minutes

SERVES: 4

675g (1½lb) small new
   potatoes, washed
1 stick celery, chopped
25g (1oz) polyunsaturated
   margarine
1 × 15ml spoon (1 tablespoon)
   toasted sesame seeds

FOR THE DIP
225g (8oz) cottage cheese
2 × 15ml spoons (2
   tablespoons) soured cream

1 × 15ml (1 tablespoon) tomato
   sauce
1 × 5ml spoon (1 teaspoon)
   dried oregano
1 × 5ml spoon (1 teaspoon)
   lemon juice
freshly ground black pepper
1 clove of garlic, crushed
   (optional)

1. Cook the potatoes. Prick each one with a sharp knife – just
   once is enough.
2. Put the potatoes and celery into a roasting bag with 2 ×
   15ml spoons (2 tablespoons) of cold water. Seal the bag
   loosely and stand it in a vegetable dish.
3. Microwave on 100%/FULL power for 10 minutes, turning
   the bag over after 5 minutes. Set aside for 10 minutes.
4. Put the margarine into a large bowl and microwave on
   40%/SIMMER for 1–2 minutes or until melted.
5. Drain the potatoes and celery and stir into the melted
   margarine. Toss to coat.
6. Turn into a serving dish and sprinkle with toasted sesame
   seeds. Serve with cocktail sticks and the dip.
7. To make the dip: Put the cottage cheese into a food processor
   or liquidizer and process until smooth.
8. Add all the remaining ingredients and process to combine.
   Turn into a small dish and chill until ready to serve.

* Do not try to toast sesame seeds in the microwave as they are not
   'bulky' enough and may cause your machine to arc or spark.

NUTTY COURGETTES

Courgettes stuffed with nuts, breadcrumbs, onion and tomato
purée make an appetizing starter that is full of fibre, protein and

taste. Suitable for vegetarians, this colourful starter may be cooked in advance and reheated when your guests arrive. To reheat, covered, will take about 4 minutes on 100%/FULL power.

PREPARATION TIME (after assembling ingredients):
   10 minutes
MICROWAVE COOKING TIME: 11–13 minutes
SERVES: 4

4 medium-sized courgettes
salt
25g (1oz) sunflower margarine
25g (1oz) brown breadcrumbs, fresh
75g (3oz) mixed nuts – walnuts, cashews, almonds – finely chopped
1 small onion, very finely chopped
1 × 15ml spoon (1 tablespoon) tomato purée
½ × 5ml spoon (½ teaspoon) dried basil

freshly ground black pepper
1–2 × 15ml spoons (1–2 tablespoons) semi-skimmed milk
2 × 15ml spoons (2 tablespoons) dry cider or dry white wine

TO SERVE
a salad garnish and a wedge of lemon for each person

1. Wash the courgettes and remove the ends from each one.
2. Cut a thin, lengthways slice from each courgette. Reserve this slice to be used as a lid.
3. Scoop out the courgette flesh, using a teaspoon, leaving a shell which will resemble a canoe.
4. Chop the flesh roughly and put it into a colander. Sprinkle the hollowed shell and flesh with salt. Set aside for 10 minutes to extract the bitter juices.
5. Rinse the shells and courgette flesh well under cold running water. Drain well and pat dry.
6. Put margarine into a 1.7 litre (3 pint) mixing bowl and microwave, uncovered, on 100%/FULL power for 1 minute. Stir in the chopped courgette flesh and the breadcrumbs, nuts, onion, tomato purée and basil. Mix well and season with black pepper. Add milk and mix to bind the ingredients together.

7. Divide the mixture between the courgette shells evenly, piling it up well.
8. Top each filled courgette with a reserved lid and put the courgette boats, close together, in a suitable shallow container. Pour the cider or wine into the base of the container.
9. Cover and microwave on 100%/FULL power for 10–12 minutes, giving the containers a ¼-turn twice during this time.
10. Allow to stand for 5 minutes, then serve with a salad garnish.

FISH

Fish is a valuable source of protein, vitamins and minerals. White fish, such as cod, halibut, plaice and whiting, have very little fat, while oily fish, like trout, mackerel, herring or sardines, have a polyunsaturated fat content (the sort doctors prefer for a healthy heart) distributed throughout their flesh. These oily fish are a good source of fat-soluble vitamins A and D.

Fish is one of the quickest foods to cook in the microwave. It should be cooked with a little liquid, and covered with a lid during cooking, to keep it moist, and the resulting fish juices should be made into a sauce to serve with the fish.

Fish freezes well and may be microwaved straight from frozen, without defrosting, in a covered dish, on 100%/FULL power. If using this method, increase the cooking times in the following recipes slightly to allow for the frozen fish.

HOT AND COLD SALAD

Crisp salad vegetables with vitamins, minerals and fibre served with hot chicken livers and mushrooms provide an unusual meal for entertaining that involves very little work. The prawns add protein and a touch of luxury, but drained tuna fish could be substituted. Serve with crusty wholemeal bread. This meal provides protein, fibre and a little fat.

PREPARATION TIME (after assembling ingredients):
20 minutes
MICROWAVE COOKING TIME: 6½ minutes
SERVES: 4

FOR THE SALAD
1 iceberg lettuce, washed and roughly shredded

1 bunch watercress, roughly chopped

1 carrot, peeled and cut into
   julienne strips
4 radishes, sliced
4 spring onions, each cut into
   strips
1 eating pear, cored and diced

TO ADD TO THE SALAD
2 × 15ml spoons (2
   tablespoons) olive oil
225g (8 oz) chicken livers,
   roughly chopped
225g (8oz) button mushrooms,
   wiped clean, sliced

150g (6oz) cooked, peeled
   prawns

FOR THE DRESSING
2 × 15ml spoons (2
   tablespoons) white wine
   vinegar
3 × 15ml spoons (3
   tablespoons) rapeseed oil
½ × 5ml spoon (½ teaspoon)
   dried parsley
freshly ground black pepper

1. Prepare the salad, using all the ingredients listed, arranging them attractively on an oval dish.
2. Pre-heat a large, deep browning dish, without its lid, for 7
   minutes on 100%/FULL power, or a small, deep browning
   dish, without its lid, for 5 minutes.
3. Put the olive oil into the heated dish and microwave on
   100%/FULL power for 1½ minutes.
4. Stir in the chicken livers and mushrooms, turning in the hot
   oil until the sizzling stops.
5. Cover and microwave on 100%/FULL power for 5 minutes,
   stirring and re-covering after 3 minutes.
6. Mix all the ingredients for the dressing and pour over the
   prepared salad. Toss to coat.
7. Remove the mushrooms and chicken livers, using a draining spoon, and arrange on the salad with the prawns. Serve
   immediately.

WHITING WITH ONIONS AND HERBS

A very simple way to cook this white fish that is high in protein
and contains hardly any fat. Whiting is a good source of calcium.
It contains only 21 calories per ounce and provides B vitamins,
so eat more whiting – you'll be doing yourself a favour.

PREPARATION TIME (after assembling ingredients):
5 minutes
MICROWAVE COOKING TIME: 4–5 minutes
SERVES: 4

1 onion, ringed
675g (1½lb) whiting fillets
1 × 5ml spoon (1 teaspoon)
dried parsley
freshly ground black pepper

3 × 15ml spoons (3
tablespoons) semi-skimmed
milk

TO GARNISH
wedges of lemon

1. Arrange the onion slices on the base of a large dish.
2. Top with the whiting fillets, in a single layer if possible.
3. Sprinkle with the parsley and season with pepper.
4. Pour over the milk and cover with a lid.
5. Microwave on 100%/FULL power for 4–5 minutes. Allow to stand, covered, for 5 minutes, then lift the whiting out with a fish slice and serve garnished with the lemon, accompanied by Potato and Parsnip au Gratin (see p. 84) and a green salad.

SMOKED HADDOCK ON TOMATOES

The lovely smoky flavour of this golden fish goes well with tomatoes. It is particularly good for you when cooked with tomatoes and a squeeze of lemon. A quickly cooked, high-protein, low-fat meal. Tomatoes provide fibre and vitamin C.

PREPARATION TIME (after assembling ingredients):
5 minutes
MICROWAVE COOKING TIME: 13–14 minutes
SERVES: 3–4

2 medium courgettes, sliced
1 × 400g can chopped
tomatoes
freshly ground black pepper
2 × 5ml spoons (2 teaspoons)
lemon juice

450g (1lb) smoked haddock
fillet
2 × 5ml spoons (2 teaspoons)
arrowroot, level

TO GARNISH
sprigs of fresh rosemary

1. Arrange the courgettes in a thin layer over the base of a casserole dish.
2. Top with the tomatoes. Season with the pepper and add the lemon juice.
3. Arrange the haddock, in a single layer, on top of the vegetables.
4. Cover and microwave on 100%/FULL power for 10 minutes.
5. Allow to stand for 5 minutes, then carefully lift the haddock on to a serving dish.
6. Mix the arrowroot to a smooth paste with a little water. Stir into the tomatoes and courgettes. Return to the microwave, uncovered, and microwave on 100%/FULL power for 3–4 minutes until boiling and thickened. Stir frequently while thickening the sauce.
7. Pour the sauce over the fish and serve immediately, garnished with the sprigs of rosemary.

* Weight-watchers may prefer not to thicken the sauce.

COD CRUMBLE

High-protein cod, rich in calcium and vitamins, is combined with hard-boiled eggs and a low-fat cheese sauce to make an appetizing meal. The crispy topping of dry bread, cheese and herbs adds carbohydrate and a delicious texture to this fish meal.

PREPARATION TIME (after assembling ingredients):
   20 minutes
MICROWAVE COOKING TIME: about 15 minutes
SERVES: 4

6 frozen cod steaks, each weighing 92g (3.25oz)
2 × 15ml spoons (2 tablespoons) semi-skimmed milk

freshly ground black pepper
2 hard-boiled eggs, cooked conventionally, then plunged into cold water, shelled and chopped

FOR THE SAUCE
**25g (1 oz) polyunsaturated
margarine
30g (1¼oz) wholemeal flour
enough semi-skimmed milk to
make resulting fish juices up
to 340ml (12fl oz)
½ × 5ml spoon (½ teaspoon)
made mustard
75g (3oz) half-fat Cheddar
cheese, grated**

FOR THE CRUMBLE TOPPING
**100g (4oz) dry breadcrumbs
(see note)
25g (1oz) half-fat Cheddar
cheese, grated
1 × 5ml spoon (1 teaspoon)
dried parsley**

1. Cook the fish: Put the frozen cod steaks, in a single layer, in the bottom of a medium casserole dish.
2. Pour over the 2 × 15ml spoons (2 tablespoons) milk and season with a little black pepper.
3. Cover and microwave on 100%/FULL power for about 8 minutes, or until the fish is cooked. Set aside, covered, for 5 minutes.
4. Make the sauce: Put the margarine into a 1 litre (2pt) jug and microwave on 100%/FULL power for 45 seconds to 1 minute, or until melted. Stir in the flour.
5. Drain the liquid from the fish and measure it, making it up to 340ml (12fl oz) with semi-skimmed milk. Stir this gradually into the fat and flour, blending the first addition of liquid really well with a wooden spoon.
6. Microwave, uncovered, on 100%/FULL power for 4 minutes, or until boiling and thickened. Stir with a balloon whisk frequently during cooking. (The sauce will rise right up in the jug as it cooks, so the large jug is vital.)
7. Beat in the grated cheese and mustard.
8. Cut the fish into bite-sized pieces and add the hard-boiled eggs.

* To dry bread, simply cut thick slices of unsliced bread – brown, white or wholemeal. Cut each slice into four. Arrange on a baking sheet and dry out in your conventional oven when you are using it for something else. Cool and crush, but don't crush too finely for this recipe as it needs the texture of a crumble.

* For a special occasion I add 100g (4oz) peeled, cooked prawns with the hard-boiled eggs.

9. Pour the sauce over to coat.
10. Combine the ingredients for the topping and fork over to cover.
11. Microwave, uncovered, on 100%/FULL power for about 2 minutes to reheat. Serve immediately with peas and carrots.

CHEESY FISH PIE

Coley is one of the cheapest fish available. The pink/grey appearance of raw coley whitens on cooking and it is highly nutritious, like all white fish – high in protein, calcium, vitamins and minerals. The added cheese, sweetcorn and mashed potatoes make the coley and tuna into a complete meal. Serve with a tossed, mixed salad or a vegetable dish.

PREPARATION TIME (after assembling ingredients):
   20 minutes
MICROWAVE COOKING TIME: 18 minutes + grilling time
SERVES: 4

FOR THE POTATO TOPPING
675g (1½lb) potatoes, peeled and diced
3 × 15ml spoons (3 tablespoons) semi-skimmed milk
1 × 15ml spoon (1 tablespoon) tomato sauce

FOR THE FISH BASE
450g (1lb) coley, skinned and cubed
1 small onion, finely chopped
2 × 15ml spoons (2 tablespoons) semi-skimmed milk

freshly ground black pepper
50g (2oz) mature Cheddar cheese, grated
50g (2oz) frozen sweetcorn kernels
1 × 200g can tuna fish in oil, well drained
280ml (½ pint) fairly thick white sauce made with semi-skimmed milk (see p. 26)
1 × 15ml spoon (1 tablespoon) tomato sauce

1. Put the potatoes, with 3×15ml spoons (3 tablespoons) milk, into a roasting bag. Stand the bag in a 1.7 litre (3 pint) bowl and seal the opening loosely with an elastic band.
2. Microwave on 100%/FULL power for 11 minutes, turning the bag over once after 5 minutes. Set aside for 10 minutes.
3. Put the cubed coley into a casserole with the onion and 2×15ml spoons (2 tablespoons) semi-skimmed milk. Season with a little pepper.
4. Cover and microwave on 100%/FULL power for 5 minutes, or until the coley is cooked. Set aside, covered, for 5 minutes, then stir in the sweetcorn. Cover and set aside for 5 minutes.
5. Drain any juices from the fish into the sauce (see p. 26). Stir the cheese into the sauce.
6. Flake the drained tuna into the coley. Pour the sauce over the fish to coat.
7. Turn the potatoes into a bowl with any remaining milk. Mash down, then beat until fluffy, adding the tomato sauce and a little extra semi-skimmed milk, if necessary.
8. Spread the mashed potatoes over the fish to cover evenly.
9. Fork up. Microwave, uncovered, for 2 minutes on 100%/FULL power to reheat, then brown under a pre-heated grill and serve immediately.

COD AND PRAWN PASTA

A simple meal to prepare. High in protein and low in fat, fish is an easily digested food. Pasta cooks so well in the microwave, and fish is so quick to cook, that this meal is quicker to prepare than many of the so-called 'convenience' foods. Wholemeal pasta has more fibre so use it whenever possible.

PREPARATION TIME (after assembling ingredients):
  10 minutes
MICROWAVE COOKING TIME: 16 minutes
SERVES: 4

225g (8oz) pasta shapes,
  wholemeal if possible
1 onion, chopped
rind and juice of ½ a lemon
4 cod steaks, each weighing
  92g (3.25oz), defrosted if
  frozen
1 × 5ml spoon (1 teaspoon)
  dried parsley
2 × 15ml spoons (2 table-
  spoons) semi-skimmed milk

100g (4oz) cooked, peeled
  prawns
2–3 × 15ml spoons (2–3
  tablespoons) grated
  Parmesan cheese

TO GARNISH
wedges of lemon and sprigs of
  parsley

1. Put the pasta into a 2.3 litre (4 pint) casserole. Cover with boiling water.
2. Cover and microwave on 100%/FULL power for 10 minutes, stirring and re-covering once after 5 minutes.
3. Set aside, covered.
4. Put the onion into a 1.7 litre (3 pint) casserole and microwave on 100%/FULL power for 2 minutes. Stir in the lemon rind and juice.
5. Arrange the cod steaks in a single layer on the onions.
6. Sprinkle with the dried parsley. Add the milk.
7. Cover and microwave on 100%/FULL power for about 4 minutes, or until the fish is opaque.
8. Drain the pasta and rinse with boiling water. Turn the pasta into a serving dish.
9. Flake the fish and add the prawns. Turn on to the cooked pasta.
10. Sprinkle liberally with Parmesan. Garnish with lemon and parsley and serve immediately. A mixed salad is a good accompaniment for this fish dish.

MONK FISH IN CIDER SAUCE

Monk fish is known as 'poor man's scampi'. It is an ugly fish to look at, with a very large head. The succulent firm flesh may be bought as a whole fish, or as fish steaks. Like all fish it must be used when really fresh. Its food value is as for all white fish. A high-protein, well-flavoured special fish dish.

PREPARATION TIME (after assembling ingredients):
5 minutes
MICROWAVE COOKING TIME: 13–14 minutes
SERVES: 3

1 medium red pepper,
  deseeded and chopped
1 medium green pepper,
  deseeded and chopped
1 medium onion, chopped
1–2 cloves garlic, crushed
450g (1lb) monk fish fillet,
  skinned and cubed
285ml (½ pint) dry cider +
  2 × 15ml spoons (2
  tablespoons) dry cider
2 × 15ml spoons (2
  tablespoons) cornflour,
  rounded
freshly ground black pepper

a little sea-salt
2 × 15ml spoons (2
  tablespoons) frozen peas
2 × 15ml spoons (2
  tablespoons) frozen
  sweetcorn
1 × 220g (7½oz) can
  butterbeans, drained

TO SERVE
plenty of freshly chopped
  parsley *or* grated Parmesan
  cheese
cooked rice *or* pasta

1. Put the red and green peppers into a medium-sized casserole with the onion and garlic. Add 2 × 15ml spoons (2 tablespoons) dry cider. Cover and microwave on 100%/FULL power for 4 minutes. Stir.

2. Add the monk fish in a single layer.

3. Cover and microwave on 100%/FULL power for 4 minutes, stirring and re-covering after 2 minutes.

4. Mix the cornflour to a smooth paste with a little of the 285ml (½ pint) dry cider. Blend in the remainder of the cider.

5. Stir the blended cornflour into the monk fish and vegetables.

6. Season with sea-salt and pepper. Add the peas and sweet-corn.

7. Microwave, covered, on 100%/FULL power for 5–6 minutes, stirring frequently, or until the sauce boils and thickens.

8. Stir in the drained butterbeans.

9. Serve immediately on a bed of cooked rice or pasta, sprinkled with freshly chopped parsley or Parmesan cheese.

SWEET AND SOUR PRAWNS

An attractive, colourful combination of crisp, fibre-full vegetables with prawns. The honey and soya sauce give a Chinese flavour to this dish. Prawns provide protein, vitamins and minerals. A meal with virtually no fat at all.

PREPARATION TIME (after assembling ingredients):
   10 minutes
MICROWAVE COOKING TIME: 13–15 minutes
SERVES: 4

1 medium cauliflower, florets only
100g (4oz) mangetout, frozen
1 medium onion, ringed
1 red pepper, deseeded and chopped
100g (4oz) frozen sliced mushrooms
2 × 15ml spoons (2 tablespoons) light soya sauce
2 × 15ml spoons (2 tablespoons) pineapple juice

1 × 5ml spoon (1 teaspoon) runny honey
freshly ground black pepper
350g (12oz) peeled prawns
1 × 220g can pineapple pieces in natural juice, drained
2 × 5ml spoons (2 teaspoons) arrowroot, level

TO SERVE
a bed of cooked brown rice
plenty of freshly chopped parsley
spring onion curls

1. Put the cauliflower florets, frozen mangetout, onion, red pepper and mushrooms into a large casserole dish.
2. Mix together the soya sauce, pineapple juice and honey. Season with pepper. Pour over the vegetables.
3. Cover and microwave on 100%/FULL power for 8–10 minutes, stirring and re-covering twice during cooking.
4. Allow to stand, covered, for 2–3 minutes, then add the pieces of drained pineapple and the prawns.
5. Cover and microwave on 100%/FULL power for 3 minutes.
6. Drain off the liquid into a jug. Blend the arrowroot with a little water and stir into the juices in the jug.
7. Microwave on 100%/FULL power for about 2 minutes, stirring frequently.
8. Pour the sauce over the prawns and vegetables and serve

immediately on a bed of rice, sprinkled with plenty of chopped parsley and garnished with the spring onion curls.

COD IN MUSTARD SAUCE

Meaty cod steaks are very filling. I always keep a bag of frozen cod steaks, high in protein and low in calories, in the freezer. Fish can be cooked straight from frozen and takes only slightly longer than fresh fish (use FULL power and do not defrost first). The mustard sauce adds a bite to the flaky cod.

PREPARATION TIME (after assembling ingredients):
   10 minutes
MICROWAVE COOKING TIME: 13 minutes
SERVES: 4

4 × 150g (6oz) cod steaks, fresh
2 shallots, peeled and chopped
25g (1oz) polyunsaturated
   margarine
25g (1oz) wholemeal flour
285ml (½ pint) light chicken or
   vegetable stock, hot

2 × 5ml spoons (2 teaspoons)
   made mustard, level

TO GARNISH
a few capers

1. Arrange the cod in a single layer over the base of a round dish. Sprinkle over the shallots.
2. Make the sauce: Put the margarine into a 1 litre jug and microwave on 100%/FULL power for 1 minute. Stir in the flour and mustard. Gradually stir in the stock.
3. Microwave, uncovered, on 100%/FULL power for about 4 minutes, or until the sauce rises right up in the jug. Beat with a wire balloon whisk twice during this time.
4. Pour the sauce over the cod evenly. Cover and microwave on 100%/FULL power for 8 minutes, or until the fish is fork-tender.
5. Set aside, covered, for 5 minutes, then serve garnished with the capers and accompanied by jacket potatoes and courgettes.

FRUITY TROUT

Trout is classified as an oily fish, which means the fat is distributed throughout its body tissue. The fat content is 10–20% polyunsaturated fat, which is far better for us than the saturated fats found in cheese, meat, butter, eggs and milk. In this recipe the trout are stuffed with apple and cooked in orange juice, which counteracts the rich taste a little.

PREPARATION TIME (after assembling ingredients):
    10 minutes + soaking time
MICROWAVE COOKING TIME: 8 minutes
SERVES: 4

4 rainbow trout, cleaned and gutted (approximately 150g (6oz) per fish)
75g (3oz) wholemeal breadcrumbs, fresh
2 dried apricots, chopped
85ml (3fl oz) semi-skimmed milk
1 small eating-apple, peeled and grated

1 × 15ml spoon (1 tablespoon) freshly chopped parsley
2 × 5ml spoons (2 teaspoons) lemon juice
2 × 15ml spoons (2 tablespoons) orange juice

TO GARNISH
slices of fresh orange

1. Put the breadcrumbs and dried apricots into a medium-sized bowl. Pour over the milk. Cover and set aside for 20 minutes.
2. Add the prepared apple with the parsley and lemon juice. Stir well.
3. Divide the stuffing between the fish, pressing it into the cavities. Press the fish closed again.
4. Arrange the fish, in a single layer, nose to tail in a suitable dish.
5. Pour over the orange juice.
6. Cover and microwave on 100%/FULL power for about 8 minutes.
7. Allow to stand for 5 minutes, then serve garnished with fresh orange and accompanied by scalloped potatoes and broccoli.

TOMATO PLAICE FILLETS

Fish, cooked with healthy ingredients instead of the fat used in, for example, frying, is one of the best protein foods available. Cooked quickly in the microwave it is such a simple meal to serve and is vastly underused. Fish is now readily available, fresh and frozen; it is extremely versatile and there is very little waste.

PREPARATION TIME (after assembling ingredients):
   15 minutes
MICROWAVE COOKING TIME: 6–8 minutes
SERVES: 4

8 small plaice fillets

FOR THE STUFFING
2 × 15ml spoons (2 tablespoons) fresh wholemeal breadcrumbs, rounded
100g (4oz) button mushrooms, finely chopped
freshly ground black pepper
2 × 5ml spoons (2 teaspoons) lemon juice

2 × 5ml spoons (2 teaspoons) tomato purée
semi-skimmed milk for mixing
450g (1lb) tomatoes, peeled and sliced
1 × 5ml spoon (1 teaspoon) dried mixed herbs

TO GARNISH
wedges of lemon

1. Prepare the stuffing: Put the breadcrumbs and mushrooms into a bowl. Season with a little pepper.
2. Add the lemon juice and tomato purée and just enough milk to moisten. Mix well.
3. Lay each plaice fillet out flat and divide the stuffing between them. Spread over to cover fairly thinly.
4. Roll the fillets up.
5. Arrange the sliced tomatoes over the base of a serving dish, – a 20cm (8in) pottery quiche dish is ideal. Top with herbs. Season with a little pepper.
6. Lift the prepared plaice on to the tomatoes. Arrange them close together so that they will not uncurl. Secure with wooden cocktail sticks, if necessary.

7. Cover and microwave on 100%/FULL power for about 6–8 minutes, or until the fish are cooked.
8. Allow to stand, covered, for 5 minutes. Then serve garnished with lemon wedges, with jacket potatoes and broccoli.

* As an alternative method of serving, the plaice may be lifted from the tomatoes after the standing time and set aside, covered. Mix 2 × 5ml spoons (2 teaspoons) arrowroot to a smooth paste and stir in to the tomatoes and their liquid. Microwave, uncovered, on 100%/FULL power for 1–2 minutes, or until thickened and boiling. Stir frequently. Lift the fish back on to the tomatoes and garnish with lemon before serving.

MUSTARD HERRINGS

Herrings are a good source of vitamins A and D, like all oily fish. Cooked in apple juice and served with apple sauce, they need only a green salad and wholemeal bread to make a complete supper dish – quicker and easier to cook than many so-called 'convenience' foods. A high-protein meal.

PREPARATION TIME (after assembling ingredients):
    15 minutes
MICROWAVE COOKING TIME:
    8 minutes
SERVES: 4

4 fresh herrings, about 275g (10oz) each
2 × 15ml spoons (2 tablespoons) coarse-grain mustard
3 × 15ml spoons (3 tablespoons) apple juice

sprigs of fresh thyme

TO SERVE
apple sauce (see p. 65)

1. Cut the heads and tails off the fish and remove the backbones. Flatten each fish and divide the mustard between them, spreading it over evenly.

63

2. Roll the herrings up, head to tail, and arrange close together in a suitable dish. Secure with cocktail sticks, if necessary.
3. Pour over the apple juice and arrange a few sprigs of fresh thyme on the fish.
4. Cover and microwave on 100%/FULL power for about 8 minutes.
5. Allow to stand for 5 minutes, then serve with the hot apple sauce.

HERRINGS IN TOMATO JUICE

High in protein and rich in vitamins A and D and the B group, herrings are a valuable contribution to a healthy diet. Herrings contain 10–20% fat, distributed through the flesh, but it contains a higher proportion of polyunsaturated fat than the fat found in other animal foods, so oily fish may also be included in a healthy diet.

PREPARATION TIME (after assembling ingredients):
10 minutes
MICROWAVE COOKING TIME: 5–6 minutes
SERVES: 4

4 fresh, medium-sized
 herrings
1 medium onion, chopped
1 eating apple, peeled and
 diced

1 × 15ml spoon (1 tablespoon)
 finely chopped parsley
5 × 15ml spoons (5
 tablespoons) tomato juice
freshly ground black pepper

1. Cut the heads and tails off the fish and remove the backbone.
2. Arrange the onion and apple in the base of a medium-sized casserole dish.
3. Lay the herrings on top, in a single layer.
4. Sprinkle over the parsley. Season with pepper and pour over the tomato juice.
5. Cover and microwave on 100%/FULL power for 5–6 minutes.

6. Allow to stand for 5 minutes, then serve with potatoes and a cauliflower dish.

TANGY APPLE SAUCE

Apples cooked with a little lemon rind and juice have a wonderfully fresh, sherbety taste, which contrasts well with the mustardy herrings. Sweeten with just a little honey when warm so that you get the right sweet/sour taste to serve with the fish. A healthy sauce with plenty of fibre.

> PREPARATION TIME (after assembling ingredients):
>   12 minutes
> MICROWAVE COOKING TIME: 6–7 minutes
> SERVES: 4 (as an accompaniment)

750g (1½lb) Bramley cooking apples, peeled, cored and sliced	**grated rind and juice of ½ a lemon** **honey to taste**

1. Put the apples into a 1.7 litre (3 pint) mixing bowl. Add the lemon rind and juice.
2. Cover and microwave on 100%/FULL power for 6–7 minutes, stirring and re-covering after 4 minutes.
3. Stir and set aside, covered, for 15 minutes. Then add just enough honey to sweeten slightly.
4. Serve immediately with the herrings.

FISH FLAN

The flan case is made from wholewheat flour, which adds fibre and carbohydrate to the high-protein fish. A good way to use one of the cheaper types of fish.

> PREPARATION TIME (after assembling ingredients):
>   20 minutes
> MICROWAVE COOKING TIME: about 16–18 minutes
> SERVES: 6

FOR THE FLAN CASE
175g (6oz) wholewheat flour
75g (3oz) polyunsaturated margarine
25g(1oz) half-fat Cheddar cheese, grated
a little cayenne pepper

FOR THE FILLING
225g (8oz) coley, skinned and filleted
2 × 15ml spoons (2 tablespoons) semi-skimmed milk
freshly ground black pepper

FOR THE SAUCE
25g (1oz) polyunsaturated margarine

40g (1½oz) wholewheat flour
300ml (½ pint) semi-skimmed milk
1 × 5ml spoon (1 teaspoon) made mustard
2 × 15ml spoons (2 tablespoons) frozen sweetcorn kernels
75g (3oz) half-fat Cheddar cheese, grated

TO SERVE
paprika pepper

TO GARNISH
1–2 tomatoes, cut into rings

1. Make the flan case: Rub the fat into flour to resemble fine breadcrumbs and fork in the grated cheese with a little cayenne.

2. Mix to a dough with cold water. Knead lightly and set aside to rest for 15 minutes.

3. Roll the pastry out on a lightly floured surface and use to line a 22.5cm (9in) flan dish. Prick the sides and base with a fork.

4. Using a single strip of foil, about 2.5cm (1in) wide, line the inner sides of the flan dish. Put two sheets of absorbent kitchen paper into the base and weigh them down with some dried pasta shapes.

5. Microwave on 100%/FULL power for 4 minutes. Remove the paper, tin foil and pasta shapes and return the flan to microwave for 1–2 minutes on 100%/FULL power. Set aside.

6. Cook the fish: Arrange the coley in a single layer in a suitable shallow dish. Pour over the milk. Season with pepper.

7. Cover and microwave on 100%/FULL power for 4 minutes, or until the fish is cooked. Set aside for 5 minutes, then make the sauce:

8. Put the margarine into a 1 litre jug. Microwave, un-covered, on 100%/FULL power for 45 seconds to 1 minute, or until melted and hot.

9. Stir in the flour, then stir in the juices from the fish and the semi-skimmed milk and the mustard.

10. Microwave, uncovered, on 100%/FULL power for 4 min-utes, or until the sauce rises right up in the jug, boils and thickens. Beat well and frequently with a balloon whisk.

11. Beat in the sweetcorn and cheese.

12. Cut the fish into bite-sized pieces and fold into the sauce. Turn into the prepared flan dish.

13. Microwave, uncovered, on 100%/FULL power for 2–3 min-utes to reheat, then serve garnished with the tomato rings and seasoned with a little paprika.

FISH SOUP

Full of flavour and almost a meal on its own, this high-protein, filling soup has very little fat. It is easily digested and popular at supper parties served with a selection of cheeses and wholemeal bread. It may be prepared in advance and reheated in the microwave when your guests arrive.

PREPARATION TIME (after assembling ingredients): 15 minutes

MICROWAVE COOKING TIME: 13–14 minutes

SERVES: 4–6

1 × 15ml spoon (1 tablespoon) olive oil

1 large onion, peeled and chopped

1 clove garlic, chopped

2 tomatoes, peeled and chopped

675g (1½lb) mixed white fish (cod, whiting, haddock), skinned, filleted and roughly chopped

1.1 litre (2 pints) boiling fish or chicken stock

100g (4oz) peeled prawns

TO SERVE
freshly chopped parsley

1. Put the oil into a 2.3–2.8 litre (4–5 pint) casserole. Microwave, uncovered, on 100%/FULL for 1 minute.
2. Stir in the onion and garlic. Microwave, uncovered, on 100%/FULL power for 2–3 minutes, stirring and re-covering after 1 minute.
3. Add the tomatoes and the roughly chopped white fish with the boiling stock.
4. Cover and microwave on 100%/FULL power for 10 minutes. Stir in the prawns.
5. Allow to stand, covered, for 5 minutes, then serve sprinkled with plenty of chopped parsley.

TOMATO MACKEREL

Mackerel is an attractive fish with blue markings on its back. This recipe is delicious hot or cold. High in protein, mackerel is categorized as an oily fish containing 10–20% polyunsaturated fats – the sort that doctors recommend we should eat more of.

PREPARATION TIME (after assembling ingredients): 15–20 minutes

MICROWAVE COOKING TIME: 8 minutes

SERVES: 4

4 fresh mackerel
2 spring onions, finely chopped
1 medium-sized tomato, peeled and chopped
1 × 5ml spoon (1 teaspoon) dried chopped chives
50g (2oz) fresh brown breadcrumbs

2 cloves garlic, crushed
5 × 15ml spoons (5 tablespoons) tomato juice
freshly ground black pepper

TO GARNISH
a few chopped chives
1 tomato, peeled and sliced

1. Prepare the fish: Cut off the heads and tails, remove the backbone, and discard.
2. Make the stuffing: Put the onion and tomato into a medium bowl. Add the chives, breadcrumbs and garlic. Season with

pepper and mix well. Add 1 × 15ml (1 tablespoon) tomato juice to bind the ingredients together.

3. Divide the stuffing between the flattened mackerel, spreading it over evenly.

4. Roll each fish up, from head to tail, and arrange close together in a suitable oval dish.

5. Make small incisions in the side of each fish with a sharp knife to help it cook.

6. Pour over the remaining tomato juice. Season with a little more pepper.

7. Cover and microwave on 100%/FULL power for about 8 minutes. Allow to stand, covered, for 5 minutes, then serve garnished with the tomato slices and a few extra snipped chives. Serve with a salad and new potatoes.

FISH LOAF

An economical way to serve fish. The cod cheek and prawns provide protein, minerals and vitamins and the bread adds some carbohydrate and fibre. Serve hot with a sauce or cold with salad.

PREPARATION TIME (after assembling ingredients): 20 minutes

MICROWAVE COOKING TIME: 10–12 minutes

SERVES: 4–6

450g (1lb) cod cheek or cod fillet
50g (2oz) fresh brown breadcrumbs
50g (2oz) peeled prawns
1 × 15ml spoon (1 tablespoon) freshly chopped parsley

2 anchovy fillets, from a can, drained (optional)
1 egg, size 2, beaten
freshly ground black pepper
2 × 5ml spoons (2 teaspoons) lemon juice

1. Cut the fish into very small pieces, using scissors – discard any very tough skin, but leave the rest. Put the fish into a medium-sized mixing bowl.

2. Add the breadcrumbs, prawns and parsley, and the chopped anchovy fillets, if used. Mix well.
3. Add the beaten egg with the black pepper and lemon juice. Mix really well.
4. Turn into a 1.7 litre (3 pint) plastic, reusable, microwave bread-baker. Level the surface.
5. Microwave, covered, on 70%/ROAST for 10–12 minutes, giving the container a ½-turn after 3 minutes and again after 6 minutes.
6. Allow to stand for 5 minutes, then turn out and serve with a parsley sauce (see note).

* Use the recipe for Mustard Sauce on p. 77 but omit the mustard and gently stir in 1–2 × 15ml spoons (1–2 tablespoons) finely chopped parsley at the end of the cooking time.

HADDOCK IN PARSLEY MAYONNAISE

Cooked fish is delicious served cold. The mayonnaise has a fair amount of fresh parsley added to it, which makes it a reasonable source of vitamin C. The mayonnaise adds polyunsaturated fat, so served with bread or boiled potatoes this dish forms a well-balanced meal for four.

PREPARATION TIME (after assembling ingredients): 20 minutes
MICROWAVE COOKING TIME: 8 minutes
SERVES: 4

450g (1lb) fresh haddock, skinned and filleted
1 × 15ml spoon (1 tablespoon) lemon juice + 1 × 15ml spoon (1 tablespoon) water
½ × 5ml spoon (½ teaspoon) dried basil or 2 sprigs of fresh basil

FOR THE MAYONNAISE
1 egg, size 3
1 egg yolk
a little sea-salt

freshly ground black pepper
250ml (½ pint) olive oil
2 × 15ml spoons (2 tablespoons) freshly chopped parsley
1 × 15ml spoon (1 tablespoon) white wine vinegar

TO ADD TO THE COLD FISH
50g (2oz) green or pimento olives (stoned, if using green)

100g (4oz) **button mushrooms,**
   sliced
75g (3oz) **frozen sweetcorn**
   kernels

TO GARNISH
slices of lemon

1. Arrange the fish in a single layer in a suitable large dish. Spoon over the mixed lemon juice and water. Sprinkle over the dried basil, or lay the fresh basil on top of the fish.
2. Cover and microwave on 100%/FULL power for about 6 minutes, or until the fish is cooked. Set aside, covered, until completely cold.
3. Meanwhile make the mayonnaise: Put the egg yolk and egg into the food processor or liquidizer (use the metal blade if using a food processor). Add a little sea-salt and some freshly ground black pepper.
4. Process for about 5 seconds, then, with the machine running, gradually add the oil, very slowly at first, and then a little faster, until the mayonnaise is thick and creamy. Add the vinegar to reduce the thickness of the mayonnaise a little and process just to mix. Add the parsley and process just to mix again.
5. Flake the cold fish into a bowl, discarding any cooking liquid. Add the halved olives and the mushrooms.
6. Microwave the sweetcorn in a bowl, covered, on 100%/FULL power for 2 minutes.
7. Stir and turn into a sieve. Refresh under cold running water. Drain well and turn on to the fish.
8. Add the mayonnaise and stir gently with a metal spoon.
9. Serve on a bed of crisp lettuce and cucumber, garnished with slices of lemon.

WHITING WITH LEEKS AND COURGETTES

High-protein whiting, cooked on a bed of leeks and courgettes with orange, develops a beautiful flavour. This no-fat recipe is garnished with fresh orange slices and fresh basil. Plenty of fibre and protein!

PREPARATION TIME (after assembling ingredients):
   10 minutes
MICROWAVE COOKING TIME: 17–22 minutes
SERVES: 4

450g (1lb) leeks, cleaned and
   ringed
2 medium courgettes, sliced
4 large fillets whiting
1 stick celery heart, finely
   chopped
3 × 15ml spoons (3
   tablespoons) orange juice
freshly ground black pepper
½ × 5ml spoon (½ teaspoon)
   made mustard

142ml (¼ pint) milk
1 × 15ml spoon (1 tablespoon)
   cornflour, rounded
75g (3oz) well-flavoured
   Cheddar cheese

TO SERVE
1 large orange, peeled and
   segmented
fresh basil

1. Put the leeks and courgettes into the base of a large dish.
2. Arrange the whiting, in a single layer, on top of the veg-
    etables.
3. Sprinkle the celery over the fish. Pour over the orange juice
    and season with a little black pepper.
4. Cover and set aside for 10 minutes, then microwave on
    100%/FULL power for 10–12 minutes, or until the fish is
    cooked.
5. Using a fish slice, carefully lift off the fish fillets and
    transfer to a warmed serving dish.
6. Tip the vegetables and any juices into a 3 pint bowl. Add the
    made mustard and the milk.
7. Cream 1 rounded tablespoon cornflour with a little milk and
    add.
8. Microwave on 100%/FULL power for 7–10 minutes, stirring
    frequently. The sauce will thicken and the courgettes will
    finish cooking.
9. Beat in 3oz grated cheese. Serve with the fish, garnished
    with the basil and segmented orange.

KIPPER PÂTÉ

Kippers, an excellent source of protein, vitamins, minerals and polyunsaturated fats, are a wonderfully flavoured, smoky fish. This pâté is made with quark – a low-fat creamy cheese – horseradish and semi-skimmed milk. A pleasant, light pâté which is always popular.

PREPARATION TIME (after assembling ingredients):
    10 minutes
MICROWAVE COOKING TIME: 3 minutes
SERVES: 4

1 × 200g (7.05oz) packet boil-in-the-bag Scottish kippers	freshly ground black pepper 1 × 15ml spoon (1 tablespoon) creamed horseradish sauce
75g (3oz) quark (skimmed-milk soft cheese)	3 × 15ml spoons (3 tablespoons) skimmed milk

1. Pierce the bag of kippers once and lay on a plate. Microwave on 100%/FULL power for 3 minutes, turning the bag over once after 1½ minutes. Set aside until cold.
2. Flake the kippers into a food processor or liquidizer, discarding the skin. Add the quark, pepper and creamed horseradish. Process or liquidize to combine.
3. With the machine running, gradually add the milk until the correct consistency results.
4. Turn into a pâté dish and serve with toasted wholemeal bread.

BROWN RICE KEDGEREE

A complete meal, excellent served at any time of the day. Protein, carbohydrate, vitamins, minerals and fibre are all present in this colourful dish. Serve hot or cold.

When cooking large pieces of haddock, cut the fish in half and arrange the tails towards the centre of the dish.

PREPARATION TIME (after assembling ingredients):
   15 minutes
MICROWAVE COOKING TIME: 37 minutes
SERVES: 4

450g (1lb) smoked haddock
2 × 15ml spoons (2
   tablespoons) semi-skimmed
   milk
1 medium onion, chopped
225g (8oz) brown rice
1 × 5ml spoon (1 teaspoon)
   ground turmeric
550ml (1 pint) boiling fish
   stock

2 hard-boiled eggs, cooked
   conventionally, then
   chopped
plenty of freshly chopped
   parsley

TO GARNISH
wedges of lemon

1. Lay the smoked haddock, in a single layer, in a suitable
    dish. Pour over the milk.
2. Cover and microwave on 100%/FULL power for 5 minutes,
    or until the fish is cooked. Set aside, covered.
3. Put the onion into a 2.3–2.8 litre (4–5 pint) casserole and
    microwave, covered, on 100%/FULL power for 2 minutes.
4. Stir in the rice and turmeric and add the boiling stock.
5. Cover and microwave on 100%/FULL power for 30 minutes.
    Do not open the door at all during this time. Allow to stand,
    covered, for 10 minutes.
6. Fluff up the rice, adding the flaked haddock and the hard-
    boiled eggs with the parsley.
7. Turn on to a serving dish and serve immediately, garnished
    with the wedges of lemon.

*   Should this dish need reheating, simply cover the serving dish with
    clingfilm and microwave on 100%/FULL power for about 2 minutes,
    or until heated through.

SIMPLE COD STEAKS

I am often asked how to cook fish for babies. Here is a simple and
completely straightforward way of dealing with frozen cod
steaks, which are high in protein, contain hardly any fat, and

have calcium, a little iron and the B group of vitamins. This recipe is also ideal for convalescents and the elderly.

> PREPARATION TIME (after assembling ingredients): 5 minutes
> MICROWAVE COOKING TIME: 8–15 minutes
> SERVES: 4 small adult portions

4 × 95g (3.25oz) frozen cod steaks

2 × 15ml spoons (2 tablespoons) semi-skimmed milk, or water

a few snipped fresh herbs (optional)

1. Split open the packets and arrange in ring fashion on a large dinner-plate or in a shallow dish.
2. Microwave on 40%/SIMMER for 5–7 minutes, turning each packet over once after 3 minutes.
3. Set aside for 5 minutes to complete defrosting.
4. Remove the cod steaks from their packets and arrange in ring fashion on a plate or dish.
5. Pour over the milk or water and sprinkle with herbs, if they are being used.
6. Cover with clingfilm and microwave on 100%/FULL power for 3–5 minutes.
7. Allow to stand for 5 minutes before serving.

* These cod steaks may be cooked straight from frozen on 100%/FULL power, but I prefer the result if they are defrosted first.

VEGETABLES AND SALADS

Let overcooked vegetables become a thing of the past. The microwave must be the very best method of cooking vegetables to perfection. Using the minimum of liquid and no salt, vegetables are steamed – the nutrients, colour and flavour remain in the vegetables instead of being thrown away in the cooking liquid, and the fantastic speed at which the microwave cooks vegetables so perfectly must be experienced to be believed. No messy pans to wash up afterwards either, as vegetables are cooked in a roasting bag, standing in a dish or directly in the serving dish itself.

Make more of vegetables and salads – use lemon juice and herbs to enhance them and add rice, pulses and pasta to extend them into healthy main meals, so cutting down on less healthy ingredients like meat, cheese and eggs, with their hidden fat. Vegetables are all high in fibre, contain vitamins and minerals, are low in calories, and have only traces of fat.

BROAD BEAN AND CARROT SALAD

An attractive high-fibre salad that may be prepared in advance, and is useful as an accompaniment at a dinner party or on the buffet table. Broad beans are high in fibre, and carrots add vitamin A as well as flavour and fibre. Bean sprouts are rich in vitamins B and C.

PREPARATION TIME (after assembling ingredients):
    10 minutes
MICROWAVE COOKING TIME: 6 minutes
SERVES: 4

350g (12oz) podded broad   225g (8oz) carrots, peeled and
  beans   cut into matchsticks

2 × 15ml spoons (2
  tablespoons) apple juice
½ × 5ml spoon (½ teaspoon)
  dried mixed herbs
100g (4oz) fresh bean sprouts

FOR THE DRESSING
1 × 15ml spoon (1 tablespoon)
  olive oil
1 × 15ml spoon (1 tablespoon)
  lemon juice

1 × 15ml spoon (1 tablespoon)
  apple juice
1 clove garlic, crushed
freshly ground black pepper

TO SERVE
plenty of freshly chopped
  parsley

1. Put the carrots and broad beans into a roasting bag with the apple juice and the mixed herbs.
2. Stand the bag in a suitable dish and seal loosely.
3. Microwave on 100%/FULL power for 6 minutes, turning the bag over once after 3 minutes.
4. Allow to cool in the bag, then turn into a serving dish.
5. Add the bean sprouts.
6. Put all the ingredients for the dressing into a mug and whisk with a fork. Pour over the vegetables. Toss to coat.
7. Cover and set aside for at least an hour before serving, sprinkled with the chopped parsley.

BROAD BEANS IN MUSTARD SAUCE

A high-fibre recipe with a tangy low-fat sauce. The flaked almonds or cheese both add protein to the recipe, and the nuts give an excellent crisp texture – a nutritious garnish which is as eye-appealing as it is good to eat.

PREPARATION TIME (after assembling ingredients):
  20 minutes
MICROWAVE COOKING TIME: about 10–12 minutes
SERVES: 4

450g (1lb) podded broad beans
1 sprig of sage

FOR THE SAUCE
25g (1oz) soft margarine

25g (1oz) brown flour
1 fat clove garlic, crushed
1 × 5ml spoon (1 teaspoon)
  wholegrain mustard

425ml (¾ pint) semi-skimmed milk

TO SERVE
a few toasted flaked almonds *or* a little grated Parmesan cheese

1. Wash the beans and put them into a fairly flat, round dish. Add the sage and 2 × 15ml spoons (2 tablespoons) water.
2. Cover and microwave on 100%/FULL power for 6–7 minutes, stirring and re-covering after 4 minutes. Set aside, covered.
3. Make the sauce: Put the margarine into a 1.1 litre (2 pint) jug and microwave for 45 seconds on 100%/FULL power. Stir in the flour and then gradually stir in the milk with the garlic and mustard.
4. Microwave on 100%/FULL power for 3–4 minutes, or until the sauce rises right up in the jug, boils and thickens. Stir three times with a balloon whisk during cooking.
5. Beat in any liquid from the broad beans, removing the sage first.
6. Pour the sauce over the beans, sprinkle with Parmesan cheese or almonds, and serve immediately.

RED CABBAGE WITH CARROT AND CINNAMON

Both vegetables contain vitamin A, while cabbage has varying amounts of vitamin C and carrot a little of the B group of vitamins. This eye-appealing vegetable dish is full of fibre and flavour.

PREPARATION TIME (after assembling ingredients):
    10 minutes
MICROWAVE COOKING TIME: 12–15 minutes
SERVES: 4

450g (1lb) red cabbage
3 medium carrots, peeled and grated
grated rind of 1 orange

small piece cinnamon stick, about 2.5cm (1in) long
4 × 15ml spoons (4 tablespoons) pure orange juice

2 sprigs of fresh marjoram or
   1 × 5ml spoon (1 teaspoon)
   dried marjoram, level
freshly ground black pepper

1 × 15ml spoon (1 tablespoon)
   light soya sauce
25g (1oz) raisins

1. Prepare the vegetables: Shred the cabbage finely, discarding the stalk (this is best done on a food processor using the metal blade). Grate the carrot.
2. Put the prepared vegetables into a 1.7 litre (3 pint) casserole with the orange rind.
3. Add the cinnamon stick. Combine the orange juice, marjoram, pepper and soya sauce and add to the casserole.
4. Cover and microwave on 100%/FULL power for 12–15 minutes, stirring and re-covering after 7 minutes.
5. Stir in the raisins. Re-cover and leave to stand for 5 minutes. Serve immediately, removing the cinnamon stick.

CAULIFLOWER AND ONIONS WITH GARLIC CHEESE SAUCE

Cauliflower is high in fibre and a good source of vitamin C. Onions have a wonderful flavour that combines well with the low-fat garlic cheese sauce.

PREPARATION TIME (after assembling ingredients):
   15 minutes
MICROWAVE COOKING TIME: 14–18 minutes
SERVES: 4

1 medium-sized cauliflower,
   florets only
8 pickling onions, peeled
285ml (10fl oz) semi-skimmed
   milk
1½ × 15ml (1½ tablespoons)
   cornflour, level
1–2 cloves garlic, crushed

freshly ground black pepper
115ml (4oz) quark
   (skimmed-milk, low-fat soft
   cheese)
2 × 15ml spoons (2
   tablespoons) grated
   Parmesan cheese, level

1. Put the prepared cauliflower into a roasting bag with the onions. Add 2 × 15ml spoons (2 tablespoons) cold water.
2. Fold the opening of the bag under the vegetables to seal loosely and stand the bag in a suitable serving dish.
3. Microwave on 100%/FULL power for 8–10 minutes. Turn the bag over once after 4 minutes. Set aside.
4. Cream the cornflour with a little of the milk in a 1.7 litre (3 pint) bowl. Put the remaining milk into a jug and microwave on 100%/FULL power for 2 minutes.
5. Pour the heated milk on to the blended cornflour, stirring continuously. Season with pepper. Stir in the crushed garlic.
6. Microwave on 100%/FULL power for 3–4 minutes, or until boiled and thickened. Stir frequently.
7. Drain the cauliflower and onions, adding any liquid to the hot sauce.
8. Return the drained vegetables to the serving dish. Gradually beat the low-fat cheese into the sauce.
9. Pour the sauce over the vegetables to coat.
10. Sprinkle with Parmesan cheese and serve immediately.

* It may be necessary to pop the dish back into the microwave for 1–2 minutes on 100%/FULL power to reheat.

RICE MEDLEY

Whole-grain rice is rich in fibre and contains some protein, calcium, iron and vitamin B1. In this recipe rice is combined with healthy ingredients to provide a crunchy vegetable meal which is delicious hot or cold. Ideal as a vegetarian meal or for a buffet party.

PREPARATION TIME (after assembling ingredients):
    10 minutes
MICROWAVE COOKING TIME: 23 minutes
SERVES: 4

1 clove garlic, crushed
1 medium onion, chopped
225g (8oz) Uncle Ben's
   whole-grain rice
700ml (25fl oz) chicken or
   vegetable stock, boiling
100g (4oz) frozen button
   mushrooms

50g (2oz) frozen sweetcorn
   kernels
½ a cucumber, diced
4 tomatoes, peeled and
   chopped
50g (2oz) dried apricots,
   chopped
50g (2oz) toasted cashew nuts,
   chopped

1. Put the garlic and onion into a 2.3 litre (4 pint) casserole and microwave, covered, on 100%/FULL power for 2 minutes.
2. Stir in the rice and the boiling stock. Cover and microwave on 100%/FULL power for 17 minutes. Set aside, covered, for 10 minutes. Do not lift the lid during cooking or standing!
3. Stir in the mushrooms and sweetcorn. Cover and microwave on 100%/FULL power for 4 minutes.
4. Stir in the cucumber, tomatoes and apricots. If serving hot, serve immediately sprinkled with the toasted cashew nuts. If serving cold, add all ingredients as given except for the cucumber and nuts, which should be added to the cooled dish just before serving.

PASTA SALAD

Pasta shapes are attractive to look at, and they are also good for you, being high in fibre and containing protein. The bright colours of the pepper and courgettes mix well here with the tuna fish to present a delicious and economical salad. Tuna provides protein and vitamins A and D.

PREPARATION TIME (after assembling ingredients):
   10 minutes + salting time
MICROWAVE COOKING TIME: 15–18 minutes
SERVES: 4–6

225g (8oz) pasta bows
1 × 5ml spoon (1 teaspoon)
   corn oil
2 large courgettes, sliced

salt
1 red pepper, deseeded and
   chopped
1 large onion, ringed

2–3 basil leaves
1 × 200g (7oz) can tuna fish in
  oil, drained

FOR THE DRESSING
2 × 15ml spoons (2
  tablespoons) olive oil
1 × 15ml spoon (1 tablespoon)
  dry white wine

1 × 15ml spoon (1 tablespoon)
  white wine vinegar
freshly ground black pepper

TO SERVE
a bed of Chinese leaves

1. Put the pasta bows into a 2.3 litre (4 pint) casserole with the oil. Pour over a kettleful of boiling water. Cover and microwave on 100%/FULL power for 10–12 minutes, stirring once with the handle of a wooden spoon after 5 minutes. Set aside, covered, for 5 minutes, then rinse with plenty of cold water.

2. Slice the courgettes into a colander, sprinkle liberally with salt, top with a plate and a weight, and set aside for 15 minutes (this will extract the bitter juices). Rinse well under cold running water. Drain.

3. Put the courgettes, red pepper and onion into a medium casserole.

4. Cover and microwave on 100%/FULL power for 5–6 minutes, stirring and re-covering after 3 minutes. Stand for 2 minutes, then drain in a sieve and refresh under cold running water. Shake off excess water.

5. Drain the pasta well and turn into a serving dish. Add the drained vegetables with the snipped basil. Toss to combine.

6. Flake in the tuna fish.

7. Combine all the ingredients for the dressing and mix with a fork. Pour the dressing on to the pasta salad and toss again just before serving on a bed of Chinese leaves.

* A delicious meal when served with warm wholemeal rolls.

MUSHROOM PASTA

Wholewheat pasta has more protein than white pasta. It is also a high-fibre food. The mushrooms provide vitamin B and add a delicious flavour to the sauce. Fromage blanc is now available in many supermarkets. The *matière grasse* is the fat content in fromage blanc. Choose one that is 30% or less *matière grasse*.

PREPARATION TIME (after assembling ingredients):
     12 minutes
MICROWAVE COOKING TIME: 24–6 minutes
SERVES: 4

225g (8oz) stoneground 100% wholewheat wheat ears (shaped pasta)
1 × 15ml spoon (1 tablespoon) olive oil
2 medium onions, chopped
225g (8oz) frozen, sliced button mushrooms

285ml (10fl oz) fromage blanc
freshly ground black pepper
plenty of freshly chopped parsley *or* grated Parmesan cheese

1. Put the pasta shapes into a 2.3 litre (4 pint) casserole. Pour over a kettleful of boiling water. Add 1 × 5ml spoon (1 teaspoon) olive oil.
2. Cover and microwave on 100%/FULL power for 10 minutes, stirring and re-covering after 4 minutes. Set aside, covered, for 5 minutes, then drain and rinse with boiling water. Turn into a warmed serving dish, cover and keep warm.
3. Meanwhile put the remaining oil into a 1.7 litre (3 pint) casserole with the onions. Cover and microwave on 100%/FULL power for 5 minutes. Stir in the mushrooms and microwave, covered, on 100%/FULL power for 5 minutes.
4. Stir in the fromage blanc. Season with pepper. Continue to microwave, uncovered, on 50%/MEDIUM for 4–6 minutes, stirring frequently, or until heated through.
5. Turn the mushroom sauce on to the pasta. Sprinkle with plenty of chopped parsley or Parmesan cheese and serve immediately.

RATATOUILLE

Ratatouille is literally a stew of vegetables. This high-fibre recipe is good served hot but I prefer to make it a day in advance as the flavour is superb when the ratatouille is presented cold a day after preparation. This recipe reheats well, covered.

PREPARATION TIME (after assembling ingredients):
    15 minutes + salting time
MICROWAVE COOKING TIME: 30–35 minutes
SERVES: 4

450g (1lb) courgettes, sliced
1 large aubergine, sliced
salt
2 medium onions, chopped
2 cloves garlic, crushed
1 medium parsnip, peeled and diced

1 red pepper, deseeded and chopped
450g (1lb) tomatoes, peeled and chopped
1 × 5ml spoon (1 teaspoon) dried mixed herbs, level
freshly ground black pepper

1. Arrange the sliced courgettes and aubergines in a casserole.
2. Sprinkle each layer of vegetables liberally with salt. Top with a plate and a weight and set aside for 20 minutes. This 'salting' will draw out the bitter, indigestible juices and is well worth the extra trouble. Rinse the vegetables under cold running water.
3. Put the onions and garlic into a medium bowl with the parsnip. Cover and microwave on 100%/FULL power for 5 minutes. Stir.
4. Layer the aubergines, courgettes and red pepper into a 2.3 litre (4 pint) serving dish with the tomatoes and the onion mixture. Season each layer with black pepper and some of the mixed herbs.
5. Cover and microwave on 100%/FULL power for 25–30 minutes. After 20 minutes, using oven gloves, remove the lid and continue to microwave, uncovered, for the remainder of the time so that some of the liquid will evaporate.
6. At the end of the cooking time, cover again and allow to stand for 10 minutes before serving.

POTATO AND PARSNIP AU GRATIN

Parsnips and potatoes provide fibre and both contain carbo-hydrate. This vegetable dish is really a meal in itself and is most attractive, with its crisp topping, served with a mixed salad as a supper.

> PREPARATION TIME (after assembling ingredients):
> 20 minutes
> MICROWAVE COOKING TIME:
> 40–46 minutes + grilling time
> SERVES: 4

450g (1lb) potatoes, scrubbed clean and thinly sliced
225g (8oz) parsnips, peeled and diced

FOR THE SAUCE
1½ × 15ml spoon (1½ tablespoons) cornflour, level
285ml (½ pint) semi-skimmed milk

freshly ground black pepper
1 × 5ml spoon (1 teaspoon) dried parsley
100g (4oz) cottage cheese
75g (3oz) Cheddar cheese, grated
50g (2oz) fresh wholemeal breadcrumbs

1. Arrange the potato slices and diced parsnips, in layers, in a large gratin dish.
2. Make the sauce: Cream the cornflour with a little of the milk in a 1.7 litre (3 pint) mixing-bowl. Put the remaining milk into a jug and microwave on 100%/FULL power for 2 minutes.
3. Pour the heated milk on to the blended cornflour, stirring continuously. Season with pepper. Stir in the parsley.
4. Microwave on 100%/FULL power for 3–4 minutes, or until boiling and thickened. Stir frequently.
5. Gradually stir in the cottage cheese and 50g (2oz) of the grated Cheddar cheese.
6. Pour over the prepared vegetables.
7. Cover and microwave on 70%/ROAST for 35–40 minutes. Stir once gently and re-cover after 20 minutes (see note).
8. Allow to stand for 5 minutes, then combine the remaining

Cheddar and breadcrumbs and sprinkle evenly over the surface.
9.   Brown under a pre-heated grill and serve immediately.

* Stirring this recipe is much easier than it sounds. I use a dessert spoon and fork and carefully move the vegetables around so that those nearest the centre and those around the outside edge are more or less reversed. Remember to re-cover before continuing to cook.

POTATO AND APPLE PURÉE

Potatoes contain more carbohydrate than any other vegetable, and as we eat them in such quantity in this country their vitamin C content is beneficial. The Bramley apple lightens the dish and provides an interesting flavour.

PREPARATION TIME (after assembling ingredients):
   15 minutes
MICROWAVE COOKING TIME: 18 minutes
SERVES: 4

450g (1lb) potatoes, peeled and diced
1 × 150g (6oz) Bramley cooking apple, peeled and diced
2 × 5ml spoons (2 teaspoons) freshly chopped parsley
freshly ground black pepper
½ × 5ml spoon (½ teaspoon) grated nutmeg
1–2 × 15ml spoons (1–2 tablespoons) tomato sauce

1.   Put the potatoes and apple into a roasting bag and stand in a 1.7 litre (3 pint) bowl. Add 3 × 15ml spoons (3 tablespoons) water and seal the bag loosely with an elastic band.
2.   Microwave on 100%/FULL power for 13 minutes, turning the bag over after 7 minutes. Let stand for 5 minutes. Turn the contents of the bag into the bowl.
3.   Mash the apples and potatoes.
4.   Add the tomato sauce with the nutmeg and pepper and blend until smooth.

* Be careful when you turn the roasting bag over half-way through cooking as it will be very hot.

5.   Turn into a serving dish and cover. Microwave on 40%/
     SIMMER for 5 minutes to reheat. Serve immediately.

JACKET POTATOES WITH PINK SALMON

A wonderful winter standby, jacket potatoes are so quick to cook
in the microwave. The pink salmon and parsley provides a
nutritious filling as salmon is high in protein and rich in
vitamins A and D. This delicious recipe may be served as a lunch
or supper dish with an accompanying salad.

PREPARATION TIME (after assembling ingredients):
    5 minutes
MICROWAVE COOKING TIME: 18–19 minutes
SERVES: 4

4 × 200g (7oz) potatoes,
    scrubbed clean
1 × 439g (15½oz) can pink
    salmon, drained and skin
    and bone discarded
3 × 15ml spoons (3
    tablespoons) mayonnaise
    (see p. 71)

1 × 5ml spoon (1 teaspoon)
    dried parsley
freshly ground black pepper

TO GARNISH
sprigs of parsley or
    watercress

1.   Prick the potatoes with a fork and arrange them in a ring on
     a dinner-plate.
2.   Microwave, uncovered, on 100%/FULL power for 15
     minutes, turning each potato over half-way through the
     cooking time.
3.   Wrap in a clean tea-towel and set aside for 10 minutes to
     stand.
4.   Carefully cut the potatoes in half and scoop out the flesh.
     Put the potato flesh into a large mixing-bowl. Mash well
     with a fork.
5.   Add the prepared salmon, mayonnaise, parsley and black
     pepper. Mix to combine.

6. Pile the mixture back into the potato shells. Arrange on a serving dish.
7. Cover with clingfilm and microwave on 100%/FULL power for 3–4 minutes to reheat. Serve immediately garnished with the sprigs of parsley or watercress.

MUSHROOMS PROVENÇALE

Mushrooms contain no sugar or starch. They are cholesterol-free and have a useful vitamin B content. In this recipe they are cooked in a little olive oil with tomatoes and herbs. A delicious, nutritious vegetable dish.

PREPARATION TIME (after assembling ingredients):
  10 minutes
MICROWAVE COOKING TIME: about 10–11 minutes
SERVES: 4–6

1 × 15ml spoon (1 tablespoon) olive oil
1 medium onion, chopped
1 clove garlic, crushed
1 × 5ml spoon (1 teaspoon) lemon juice
½ × 5ml spoon (½ teaspoon) dried oregano

450g (1lb) button mushrooms, wiped clean and chopped
450g (1lb) ripe tomatoes, peeled and chopped
freshly ground black pepper
2 × 5ml spoons (2 teaspoons) cornflour, level

1. Put the oil into a 1.7 litre (3 pint) bowl and microwave, uncovered, for 45 seconds on 100%/FULL power.
2. Stir in the onion and garlic. Cover and microwave on 100%/FULL power for 2 minutes.
3. Stir in the lemon juice, oregano, mushrooms and tomatoes. Season with pepper.
4. Cover and microwave on 100%/FULL power for 6 minutes, stirring and re-covering after 3 minutes.
5. Blend the cornflour to a smooth paste with a little water and stir into the vegetables. Microwave, uncovered, on 100%/FULL power for 1–2 minutes, stirring frequently, until boiling and thickened. Serve immediately.

WINTER SALAD

A mixture of winter vegetables are microwaved and then tossed in a fresh dressing and served cold as a salad. High in fibre, this recipe will be popular for winter buffet parties.

PREPARATION TIME (after assembling ingredients):
15 minutes
MICROWAVE COOKING TIME: 10 minutes
SERVES: 4–6

FOR THE WINTER SALAD
1 small cauliflower, florets only
1 large carrot, peeled and diced
1 leek, well washed and ringed
1 medium parsnip, peeled and diced
25g (1oz) raisins
1 eating apple, Discovery or Worcester if possible, cored and diced

FOR THE DRESSING
2 × 15ml spoons (2 tablespoons) olive oil
1 × 15ml spoon (1 tablespoon) white wine vinegar
½ × 5ml spoon (½ teaspoon) dried mixed herbs
rind of ½ a lemon
1 × 5ml spoon (1 teaspoon) lemon juice
freshly ground black pepper

TO SERVE
Chinese leaves or iceberg lettuce

1. Put the prepared cauliflower, carrot, leek and parsnip into a large casserole. Add 2 × 15ml spoons (2 tablespoons) cold water.
2. Cover and microwave on 100%/FULL power for 10 minutes, stirring and re-covering after 5 minutes. Set aside for 5 minutes.
3. Make the dressing by combining all the ingredients in a mug and whisking with a fork.
4. Drain the vegetables and add the raisins. Pour the dressing over. Toss to coat. Set aside, covered, until cold.
5. Just before serving, stir in the apple and arrange on a bed of Chinese leaves or iceberg lettuce.

BAKED CABBAGE WITH MUSTARD SAUCE

Cabbage contains vitamin A, iron and calcium. The microwave is a particularly healthy method of cooking cabbage, as it is cooked in very little water, and in this recipe it is actually cooked with its own sauce as part of the recipe.

> PREPARATION TIME (after assembling ingredients): 10 minutes
>
> MICROWAVE COOKING TIME: 17 minutes
>
> SERVES: 4

1 medium-sized savoy cabbage (about 675g (1½ lb))
1 medium onion, chopped
2 × 15ml spoons (2 tablespoons) brown flour, level
285ml (½ pint) well-flavoured chicken stock, cold
2 large tomatoes, skinned and chopped
1 × 15ml spoon (1 tablespoon) coarse-grain mustard

1. Cut the cabbage into fairly thick wedges, cutting out and discarding the stalk. Arrange in a large serving dish in a single layer.
2. Add 4 × 15ml spoons (4 tablespoons) cold water. Cover and microwave on 100%/FULL power for 6 minutes. Set aside after rearranging carefully and re-covering.
3. Put the onion into a 1.7 litre (3 pint) bowl and microwave on 100%/FULL power for 2 minutes.
4. Stir and wait for a minute or two, then blend in the flour, mustard and chopped tomatoes. Stirring continuously, gradually add the stock.
5. Microwave, uncovered, on 100%/FULL power for about 4 minutes, stirring frequently, until the sauce boils and thickens. Add any liquid from the cabbage to the sauce.
6. Pour the sauce over the cabbage. Cover and microwave on 100%/FULL power for about 5 minutes, or until the cabbage is tender.
7. Allow to stand for 5 minutes, then serve.

* I use the Corningware MW10 deep browning dish, with lid, for this recipe as it is just the right size. If you cover the base of the browning dish with food and don't pre-heat, it may be used as an ordinary casserole dish.

CAULIFLOWER IN WHITE WINE

An average helping of cauliflower will supply about half the daily requirements of vitamin C. In this recipe fat in the form of olive oil is added, but only a small amount is used. The combination of tomato purée, olive oil and wine with the oregano is delicious.

PREPARATION TIME (after assembling ingredients):
  10 minutes
MICROWAVE COOKING TIME: 12–14 minutes
SERVES: 4

1 medium-sized cauliflower, florets only, weight of florets 675g (1lb 8oz)
1 large onion, chopped
2 × 15ml spoons (2 tablespoons) olive oil
2 × 15ml spoons (2 tablespoons) tomato purée

1 × 5ml spoon (1 teaspoon) dried oregano
140ml (¼ pint) white wine

TO SERVE
grated Parmesan cheese

1. Arrange the cauliflower florets in a serving dish.
2. Put the chopped onion into a small mixing bowl and microwave, covered, on 100%/FULL power for 2 minutes.
3. Add the olive oil, tomato purée, oregano and wine.
4. Pour evenly over the cauliflower.
5. Cover and microwave on 100%/FULL power for 10–12 minutes, stirring gently to move the cauliflower around twice during cooking.
6. Allow to stand, covered, for 4 minutes, then serve sprinkled with the Parmesan cheese.

VEGETABLE MEDLEY WITH CHESTNUTS

A colourful array of vegetables cooked to perfection. The chestnuts add protein to this high-fibre recipe. Sprouts provide a useful amount of vitamin C, especially in winter, when fruit is expensive.

PREPARATION TIME (after assembling ingredients):
   20 minutes
MICROWAVE COOKING TIME: 11–14 minutes
SERVES: 6

450g (1lb) fresh Brussels
   sprouts
1 large carrot, peeled and cut
   into fairly large matchsticks
1 stick celery, chopped
½ a medium cauliflower,
   florets only
1 medium-sized courgette,
   sliced

1 × 5ml spoon (1 teaspoon)
   dried mixed herbs
25g (1oz) polyunsaturated
   margarine (optional)
freshly ground black pepper
225g (8oz) can whole
   chestnuts, drained

1. Peel the sprouts and mark a cross in the base of each one.
2. Put the sprouts into a large casserole with the carrot, celery,
    cauliflower florets, courgette and herbs, and with the mar-
    garine, if used. Season with black pepper. Add 2 × 15ml
    spoons (2 tablespoons) cold water.
3. Cover and microwave on 100%/FULL power for 10–12 min-
    utes, stirring and re-covering twice during this time.
4. Allow to stand for 5 minutes, then drain off excess water
    (reserve and use in a sauce or gravy).
5. Add the drained chestnuts. Cover and microwave on
    100%/FULL power for 1–2 minutes. Serve immediately.

*   As an alternative to the chestnuts, the drained vegetables may be
    sprinkled with toasted flaked almonds just before serving.

BROCCOLI WITH YOGHURT SAUCE

A recipe that is simplicity itself to prepare but tastes rich and
creamy. Low-fat yoghurt makes a healthy sauce. An average
helping of broccoli provides over half the day's requirements of
vitamin C.

PREPARATION TIME (after assembling ingredients):
   10 minutes
MICROWAVE COOKING TIME: 16–18 minutes
SERVES: 4

450g (1lb) frozen broccoli
  spears
1 medium onion, chopped
2 × 5ml spoons (2 teaspoons)
  tomato purée
freshly ground black pepper
75g (3oz) half-fat Cheddar
  cheese, grated

150g (5fl oz) natural low-fat
  yoghurt

TO SERVE
a little paprika pepper

1. Put the broccoli into a roasting bag, then stand the bag in a vegetable dish, sealing the opening loosely with an elastic band.
2. Microwave on 100%/FULL power for 8–10 minutes, turning the bag over once after 4 minutes.
3. Set aside to stand.
4. Put the onion into a 1.7 litre (3 pint) mixing bowl. Cover and microwave on 100%/FULL power for 3 minutes, stirring and re-covering after 1 minute.
5. Stir in the tomato purée, black pepper, grated cheese and yoghurt.
6. Drain the broccoli and transfer to a clean serving dish. Top with the yoghurt sauce. Cover with clingfilm and microwave on 50%/MEDIUM for 5 minutes.
7. Sprinkle with paprika pepper and serve immediately.

LEEK AND TOMATO CRUMBLE

A high-fibre dish which would be excellent served with a fish meal. The crispy topping gives a nice crunchy texture to the leeks, which have a French taste. The topping also adds carbohydrate and a little fat – energy-giving foods.

PREPARATION TIME (after assembling ingredients):
  20 minutes
MICROWAVE COOKING TIME: 16 minutes
SERVES: 4

675g (1½lb) leeks, well washed
  and sliced

1 × 400g (14oz) can chopped
  tomatoes, with herbs

1 clove garlic, crushed

FOR THE CRUMBLE
50g (2oz) polyunsaturated
  margarine
100g (4oz) fresh brown
  breadcrumbs

25g (1oz) oatmeal
25g (1oz) cashew nut kernels,
  chopped
25g (1oz) grated Cheddar
  cheese

1. Prepare the topping: Put the margarine into a 1.7 litre
   (3 pint) mixing bowl and microwave on 100%/FULL power
   for about 1½ minutes, or until melted.
2. Stir in the breadcrumbs, oatmeal and cashew nuts. Mix
   really well with a fork so that the dry ingredients absorb the
   melted margarine evenly.
3. Microwave, uncovered, on 100%/FULL power for 2½ minutes. Stir well with a fork.
4. Microwave, uncovered, on 100%/FULL power for 2 minutes.
   Break down again with a fork. Set aside, uncovered.
5. Put the leeks into a suitable dish. Pour over the tomatoes
   and add the garlic.
6. Cover and microwave on 100%/FULL power for 10 minutes,
   or until the leeks are just tender. Stir once after 4 minutes.
7. Allow the vegetables to stand for 5 minutes, then fork the
   cheese into the crispy topping. Spoon on to the vegetables to
   cover and serve immediately.

MIXED VEGETABLE STEW

As the microwave takes varying amounts of time to cook different vegetables, this nutritious recipe takes the headache out
of serving a variety of vegetables and keeping them all hot until
the complete meal is ready to be served. Fibre, protein, vitamins
and minerals are all present in this colourful dish.

PREPARATION TIME (after assembling ingredients):
  10 minutes + salting time
MICROWAVE COOKING TIME: 20–25 minutes
SERVES: 4–6

94

450g (1lb) courgettes, sliced	140ml (¼ pint) light chicken
350g (12oz) aubergine, diced	stock
salt	1 × 15ml spoon (1 tablespoon)
225g (8oz) carrots, diced	freshly chopped parsley
1 small parsnip, diced	freshly ground black pepper
1 green pepper, sliced	1 × 15ml spoon (1 tablespoon)
1 medium onion, ringed	tomato purée
100g (4oz) celery, chopped	1 × 220g (7.75oz) can
100g (4oz) mushrooms, sliced	butterbeans, drained

1. Put the courgettes and aubergines into a colander, sprinkling each layer with salt. Top with a tea-plate and stand a weight on top. Set aside for 15 minutes to extract the bitter juices.

2. Rinse the courgettes and aubergines well under cold running water. Drain and put into a 2.3 litre (4 pint) casserole dish.

3. Add the diced carrot, green pepper, onion rings, celery, parsnip and mushrooms.

4. Pour in the stock with the parsley. Season with the black pepper and add the tomato purée. Stir.

5. Cover with a lid and microwave on 100%/FULL power for 20–25 minutes. Stir and re-cover after 10 minutes and again after 15 minutes.

6. Stir in the drained butterbeans. Cover and allow to stand for 5 minutes before serving.

* To make this vegetable stew into a complete meal, simply add a little extra protein – some shelled prawns, grilled kidneys or cold sliced chicken would be ideal.

BRAISED CELERY WITH CHIVES

Celery is far quicker to braise in the microwave and the flavour is superb. Celery is high in fibre, but as it has little other food value it should be served with a sauce and a high-protein food.

PREPARATION TIME (after assembling ingredients):
15 minutes

MICROWAVE COOKING TIME: 22–4 minutes
SERVES: 4

1 head celery
1 × 15ml spoon (1 tablespoon)
 snipped chives
285ml (½ pint) vegetable or
 chicken stock, warm
a little semi-skimmed milk

1 × 15ml (1 tablespoon)
 cornflour, rounded
2 cloves garlic, crushed
freshly ground black pepper
3 rashers streaky bacon, rind
 removed

1. Clean the celery and cut into 5cm (2in) lengths. Arrange in a shallow dish.
2. Add the chives. Pour over the stock. Cover and microwave on 100%/FULL power for about 15 minutes, or until the celery is tender. Remove the lid and stir the celery once, after 7 minutes. Then re-cover.
3. Set aside for 5 minutes, then carefully pour any liquid into a 1.1 litre (2 pint) jug. Make the liquid up to 400ml (14fl oz) with the milk. Cover the celery and keep warm.
4. Microwave the jug of liquid, uncovered, for 3 minutes on 100%/FULL power.
5. Cream the cornflour with a little milk until it is a smooth paste – use a 1.7 litre (3 pint) bowl.
6. Pour the heated liquid on to the mixed cornflour, stirring continuously. Season with a little black pepper. Add the crushed garlic.
7. Microwave, uncovered, on 100%/FULL power for 2–3 minutes, or until the sauce boils and thickens. Stir frequently.
8. Pour the sauce over the cooked celery. Cover and keep warm.
9. Arrange the bacon on two sheets of absorbent kitchen paper, on a dinner-plate. Cover with another sheet of paper.
10. Microwave on 100%/FULL power for 2–3 minutes, or until starting to crisp. Set aside for 2–3 minutes.
11. Snip the cooked bacon over the celery dish just before serving – I find it easy to do this if I use scissors.

MUSHROOMS ON TOAST

Mushrooms are combined with bacon to produce a delicious snack. Bacon contains fat and protein and gives a wonderful flavour to the recipe. Serve on toasted wholemeal bread. A quick lunch or supper dish.

PREPARATION TIME (after assembling ingredients):
   5–10 minutes
MICROWAVE COOKING TIME: 8 minutes
SERVES: 4

450g (1lb) flat mushrooms, wiped clean and sliced
125g (5oz) lean unsmoked streaky bacon, de-rinded and chopped

2 cloves garlic, crushed
freshly ground black pepper
1 × 5ml spoon (1 teaspoon) dried parsley

1. In a 1.7 litre (3 pint) bowl mix together the mushrooms, bacon and garlic. Season with a little pepper. Add the parsley.
2. Cover and microwave on 100%/FULL power for about 8 minutes, stirring and re-covering after 4 minutes.
3. Serve immediately on hot toast.

LEMON COURGETTES

Although courgettes have little food value besides adding fibre to the diet, they have the most delicious flavour. This recipe is a simple combination of lemon, herbs, courgettes and polyunsaturated margarine. The courgettes should be served with a 'bite'. This vegetable dish is also good cold.

PREPARATION TIME (after assembling ingredients):
   5 minutes + salting time
MICROWAVE COOKING TIME: 9–12 minutes
SERVES: 4

450g (1lb) courgettes, sliced
salt
1 × 15ml spoon (1 tablespoon)
  olive oil

rind and juice of ½ a lemon
1 × 5ml spoon (1 teaspoon)
  dried mixed herbs

1. Arrange the courgettes in a colander, sprinkling each layer with salt. Cover with a plate and set aside for 15 minutes.
2. Rinse the courgettes under cold running water and drain dry on absorbent kitchen paper.
3. Pre-heat a small deep browning dish without the lid for 4 minutes on 100%/FULL power or a large browning dish for 7 minutes on 100%/FULL power.
4. Put the oil on to the hot dish.
5. Carefully add the courgettes, stirring with a wooden spoon until the sizzling stops.
6. Add the lemon rind and juice with the mixed herbs. Cover with the lid and microwave on 100%/FULL power for 5 minutes, stirring and re-covering after 2 minutes. Stir and serve.

CARROT AND SPROUT MEDLEY

A colourful combination of vegetables, cooked together. Vitamin A in carrots and vitamin C in sprouts are vital in winter months, when some vegetables are hard to come by. The chestnuts add protein and flavour to this vegetable dish.

PREPARATION TIME (after assembling ingredients):
  15 minutes
MICROWAVE COOKING TIME: 8 minutes
SERVES: 4

450g (1lb) fresh Brussels
  sprouts, peeled
225g (8oz) carrots, peeled
freshly ground black pepper
2 × 15ml spoon (2 tablespoons)
  orange juice
½ × 5ml spoon (½ teaspoon)
  dried mixed herbs

225g (8oz) can whole
  chestnuts, drained

TO SERVE
1 fresh orange, peeled and
  segmented with no pith

1. Make a cross in the base of each sprout and put into a roasting bag. Cut the carrots into matchsticks and add to the bag with a seasoning of pepper. Add the orange juice and herbs.
2. Seal the bag loosely and stand in a vegetable dish. Microwave on 100%/FULL power for 7 minutes, turning the bag over after 3 minutes.
3. Set aside for 5 minutes.
4. Tip the vegetables into a serving dish. Add the chestnuts, stirring gently. Cover and microwave on 100%/FULL power for 1 minute.
5. Add the freshly segmented orange, decoratively, just before serving.

STUFFED AUBERGINE

Aubergines have a wonderful colour and are extremely low in calories as long as they are not fried in fat, as they are so often served. They microwave extremely well and are delicious stuffed with cheese, which adds protein to this high-fibre recipe.

PREPARATION TIME (after assembling ingredients):
    10 minutes + salting time
MICROWAVE COOKING TIME: 12–14 minutes
SERVES: 4 as a snack or 2 as a main meal

2 medium aubergines
salt
1 medium onion, chopped
75g (3oz) grated Cheddar cheese
2 × 15ml spoons (2 tablespoons) fresh breadcrumbs, rounded

2 × 15ml spoons (2 tablespoons) natural yoghurt
freshly ground black pepper

TO SERVE
paprika pepper

1. Halve the aubergines lengthways and scoop out the flesh, leaving a shell 5mm (¼in) thick. Chop the flesh roughly.
2. Sprinkle the aubergine shells and the flesh with salt and set aside for 20 minutes to extract the bitter juices.

3. Rinse the shells and flesh well and drain on absorbent kitchen paper.

4. Put the onion into a medium bowl. Cover and microwave on 100%/FULL power for 2 minutes. Stir.

5. Add the cheese, breadcrumbs and yoghurt. Season with black pepper. Add the diced aubergine flesh and stir well to combine.

6. Divide the mixture evenly between the shells.

7. Arrange the shells in a large dish.

8. Cover and microwave on 100%/FULL power for 10–12 minutes.

9. Allow to stand, covered, for 5 minutes, then lift on to a serving dish and serve with a dusting of paprika pepper and accompanied by wholemeal rolls.

BEAN SPROUT MEDLEY

A crunchy combination of flavourful vegetables. Bean sprouts, high in fibre, contain a reasonable amount of vitamin C. They are added at the end of the recipe and quickly heated through before serving.

PREPARATION TIME(after assembling ingredients): 5 minutes

MICROWAVE COOKING TIME: 11 minutes

SERVES: 4

2 cloves garlic, crushed
1 medium onion, chopped
1 carrot, peeled and cut into matchsticks
1 stick celery, cut into matchsticks
1 red pepper deseeded and chopped

1 green or yellow pepper, deseeded and chopped
½ × 5ml spoon (½ teaspoon) ground ginger
2 × 15ml spoons (2 tablespoons) light soya sauce
225g (8oz) fresh bean sprouts

1. Put the garlic, onion, carrot and celery into a large bowl. Cover and microwave on 100%/FULL power for 4 minutes.

Stir in the red and the green or yellow pepper with the ginger and soya sauce. Add 1 × 15ml spoon (1 tablespoon) water.

2. Cover and microwave on 100%/FULL power for 4 minutes. Stir.

3. Add the bean sprouts. Stir well. Cover and microwave on 100%/FULL power for 3 minutes. Stir and serve immediately.

TARRAGON CARROTS WITH ORANGE

Colourful carrots, a good source of vitamin A, have a lovely flavour that combines well with orange juice and tarragon. Serve this vegetable dish hot or cold.

PREPARATION TIME (after assembling ingredients):
   5–10 minutes
MICROWAVE COOKING TIME: 9 minutes
SERVES: 4–6

675g (1½lb) finger carrots, peeled
½ × 5ml spoon (½ teaspoon) dried tarragon

3 × 15ml spoons (3 tablespoons) pure orange juice
1 × 5ml spoon (1 teaspoon) runny honey

1. Slice the carrots and put into a roasting bag. Add the tarragon, orange juice and honey. Seal the bag loosely with an elastic band and stand in a casserole dish.

2. Microwave on 100%/FULL power for 9 minutes, turning the bag over after 4 minutes. Set aside for 4 minutes, then serve hot.

3. If serving cold, allow to stand in the roasting bag until cold, then turn into a casserole dish to serve.

PARSNIPS WITH BACON AND WALNUTS

Parsnips contain carbohydrate and therefore provide energy. Their flavour combines well with the bacon and walnuts, both of which contain protein. The bacon should be cooked on a rack so that much of the fat will drain away.

> PREPARATION TIME (after assembling ingredients):
>   5–10 minutes
> MICROWAVE COOKING TIME: about 10 minutes
> SERVES: 4

500g (1lb 4 oz) parsnips, peeled and cut into matchsticks
3 × 15ml spoons (3 tablespoons) chicken or vegetable stock or dry cider
2 × 5ml spoons (2 teaspoons) dried parsley

freshly ground black pepper
1 rasher collar bacon, rind removed
75g (3oz) walnuts, chopped

1. Put the parsnips into a medium casserole dish. Pour over the stock or cider. Add the parsley. Season with a little black pepper.
2. Cover and microwave on 100%/FULL power for 8 minutes, stirring and re-covering after 4 minutes.
3. Set aside, covered.
4. Arrange the bacon on a microwave roasting rack or on two sheets of absorbent kitchen paper. In both cases cover with another sheet of absorbent kitchen paper. Microwave on 100%/FULL power for about 1½ minutes, or until the bacon is cooked to your liking. Let it stand for 1–2 minutes.
5. Chop the bacon (easiest done using scissors) and combine with the chopped walnuts. Drain the parsnips.
6. Sprinkle the cooked parsnips with the mixed bacon and walnuts and serve immediately.

MAIN DISHES

Poultry, lean meats, pasta and rice, savoury flans, offal – the list is endless. The microwave will achieve superb results every time with these healthy main-meal recipes. All the recipes have been well balanced nutritionally and an accompanying salad or vegetable dish is suggested to serve with the dish. The latter may often be cooked during the standing time of the main meal, which will continue to increase in temperature during this time.

People are wary of reheating cooked food. However, reheating in the microwave is quite safe provided that the food is reasonably fresh and is reheated to a sufficient temperature. Test that the food towards the centre of the plate or dish is really hot before serving, and if reheating a casserole, or similar, always stir during reheating to equalize the temperature. In most cases the food should be covered during reheating.

TURKEY WITH PEPPERS AND CORN

Diced frozen turkey, low in fat and high in protein, is available from most freezer centres. In this recipe the whole meal is cooked together in one pot, making washing up quick and simple. The sweetcorn with peppers add colour and fibre to this tasty casserole.

PREPARATION TIME (after assembling ingredients):
   15 minutes
MICROWAVE COOKING TIME: 35 minutes
SERVES: 4

450g (1lb) potatoes, preferably
  new, washed and roughly
  chopped
2 carrots, peeled and diced
1 medium onion, sliced
170ml (6fl oz) well-flavoured
  chicken stock, hot
450g (1lb) frozen diced turkey,
  defrosted

1 × 15ml spoon (1 tablespoon)
  wholemeal flour, level
115ml (4fl oz) apple juice
freshly ground black pepper
sprig of fresh thyme
1 × 225g (8oz) Bramley apple,
  peeled, cored and diced
50g (2oz) frozen sweetcorn
  with peppers

1. Put the potatoes, carrots and onion into a 2.3 litre (4 pint) casserole.

2. Add the stock. Cover and microwave on 100%/FULL power for 8 minutes. Stir.

3. Toss the meat in the flour and add it to the root vegetables in the casserole. Pour over the apple juice and season with a little black pepper. Add the thyme with the diced Bramley. Stir well.

4. Cover and microwave on 100%/FULL power for 5 minutes. Stir. Continue to microwave, covered, on 40%/SIMMER for 20 minutes or until the turkey and vegetables are tender. Stir and re-cover after 10 minutes.

5. Stir in the sweetcorn with peppers. Cover and microwave on 100%/FULL power for 2 minutes.

6. Allow to stand for 5 minutes then serve (remove the thyme before serving).

*   To defrost 450g (1lb) diced turkey will take about 8 minutes using your DEFROST control. Simply put the bag of diced turkey on a plate and place in the microwave. Turn the bag over after 4 minutes and allow the turkey to stand, after defrosting, for at least 15 minutes before using.

*   A watercress and orange salad would go well with this dish and will supply useful amounts of vitamins A and C and some iron.

*   As an alternative, use diced rabbit meat instead of the turkey. Follow the recipe exactly as given.

Moussaka

Lean chuck steak, which contains less fat than mince, is used here. The meat is extended with vegetables to provide a filling meal for six people. A complete meal, high in protein and fibre.

PREPARATION TIME (after assembling ingredients):
   20 minutes
MICROWAVE COOKING TIME:
   55–6 minutes + grilling time
SERVES: 4–6

FOR THE MEAT FILLING
1 medium aubergine, diced *or*
   225g (8oz) courgettes, sliced
salt
2 medium onions, chopped
2 rashers lean back bacon,
   de-rinded and chopped
1–2 cloves garlic, chopped
350g (12oz) chuck steak,
   minced
225g (8oz) tomatoes, peeled
   and chopped
2 × 15ml spoons (2
   tablespoons) tomato purée

450g (1lb) potatoes, scrubbed
   clean and thinly sliced

FOR THE SAUCE
285ml (½ pint) semi-skimmed
   milk
2 × 15ml spoons (2
   tablespoons) cornflour, level
1 × 5ml spoon (1 teaspoon)
   dried parsley
freshly ground black pepper
50g (2oz) grated Parmesan
   cheese

1. Put the aubergine or courgette slices into a colander. Sprinkle liberally with salt and set aside while preparing the sauce (this will extract the bitter juices and make the aubergine or courgettes easier to digest).
2. Make the sauce: Use a little of the milk to cream the cornflour to a smooth paste in a 1.7 litre (3 pint) mixing bowl.
3. Put the remaining milk into a jug and microwave on 100%/FULL power for 2 minutes.
4. Pour the heated milk on to the creamed cornflour, stirring continuously, then microwave, uncovered, on 100%/FULL power for about 2 minutes, or until boiling and thickened. Stir frequently.

5. Stir in the parsley and pepper. Set aside, stirring occasionally, until ready to use.
6. Prepare the meat filling: Put the onion, bacon and garlic into a 1.7 litre (3 pint) casserole dish. Cover and microwave on 100%/FULL power for 5 minutes, stirring and re-covering after 3 minutes. Stir in the mince. Microwave, covered, on 100%/FULL power for 5 minutes. Stir in the tomatoes with the tomato purée. Season with the black pepper.
7. Rinse the aubergine or courgettes well under cold running water. Drain and add to the mince mixture. Cover and microwave on 70%/ROAST for 10 minutes, stirring and re-covering after 5 minutes. Allow to stand for 5 minutes.
8. Put a layer of meat filling into the base of a large casserole and cover with a single layer of potatoes.
9. Continue to layer in this way, finishing with a layer of potatoes.
10. Reheat the sauce for 1–2 minutes in the microwave, then beat in a little extra milk if necessary to produce a pouring consistency.
11. Pour over the potatoes and sprinkle with the Parmesan cheese.
12. Cover with clingfilm or a lid.
13. Microwave on 70%/ROAST for 30 minutes or until the potatoes are tender (test the centre ones with a pointed knife). Give the dish a ¼-turn twice during cooking.
14. Stand for 10 minutes then brown under a pre-heated grill.
15. Serve with a salad of iceberg lettuce, chopped celery, grated carrot and raisins.

SPINACH AND QUARK QUICHE

Brown flour provides fibre and gives a nutty taste to this attractive quiche. Quark is a low-fat soft cheese that combines well with the low-fat Cheddar cheese and spinach to give this savoury flan a light texture and delicious flavour. If preferred, the flan case may be baked blind conventionally and the quiche completed in the microwave.

PREPARATION TIME (after assembling ingredients):
   10 minutes
MICROWAVE COOKING TIME: 32–8 minutes
SERVES: 4

FOR THE PASTRY
150g (6oz) wholewheat flour, plain
75g (3oz) vegetable margarine, from the refrigerator
cold water to mix

FOR THE FILLING
1 small onion, chopped
1 × 227g (8oz) packet frozen chopped spinach, defrosted

150ml (¼ pint) semi-skimmed milk
100g (4oz) quark (skimmed-milk soft cheese)
3 large eggs
freshly ground black pepper
75g (3oz) low-fat Cheddar cheese, grated
2 cloves garlic, chopped

1. Make the pastry: Put the flour into a bowl and rub in the margarine, until the mixture resembles fine breadcrumbs.

2. Add sufficient cold water to form a ball of dough. Knead lightly, then roll out and use to line a 22.5cm (9in) flan-dish. Prick the sides and base with a fork.

3. Using a single strip of foil, about 2.5cm (1in) wide, line the inside sides of the flan-dish. Put two sheets of absorbent kitchen paper into the base and weigh them down with some dried pasta shapes.

4. Microwave on 100%/FULL power for 4 minutes. Remove the paper, foil and pasta shapes and return the flan to the microwave for 1–2 minutes on 100%/FULL power. Set aside.

5. Prepare the filling: Put the onion into a 1.7 litre (3 pint) mixing bowl and microwave, covered, on 100%/FULL power for 2 minutes. Stir and set aside for 2 minutes.

6. Put the defrosted spinach into a sieve and squeeze out the excess water.

7. Whisk the skimmed milk, quark and eggs together. Sea-

son. Add the spinach and onion with the grated Cheddar cheese and the garlic.

8. Microwave this custard mixture, uncovered, on 50%/ MEDIUM for 5–6 minutes or until hot. Stir every minute and at the end of the cooking time.

9. Pour the custard into the cooked pastry case. Microwave on 50%/MEDIUM for 20–24 minutes, or until set in the centre. Give the dish a ¼-turn every 5 minutes.

10. Serve warm with new potatoes and salad.

CHICKEN RISOTTO

Rice provides the B group of vitamins and two different types of rice are used here to give an attractive appearance. Brown rice contains more fibre than does white rice, and the frozen sweetcorn and peas also add fibre. Chicken is a valuable source of protein and, as the skin is removed in this recipe, the amount of fat it contains is negligible. A colourful and nutritious main meal.

PREPARATION TIME (after assembling ingredients):
   30 minutes
MICROWAVE COOKING TIME: 32–4 minutes
SERVES: 4

3 chicken portions, about 275g (10oz) each, skinned
juice of ½ a lemon
½ × 5ml spoon (½ teaspoon) dried mixed herbs
1 medium onion, chopped
1 stick celery, chopped
1 medium red pepper, deseeded and chopped
100g (4oz) brown rice
100g (4oz) long-grain white rice

425ml (¾ pint) chicken stock, boiling
½ glass dry white wine
50g (2oz) frozen sweetcorn
50g (2oz) frozen peas
1 × 400g (1 × 14oz) can chopped tomatoes

TO SERVE
plenty of freshly chopped parsley

1. Arrange the chicken pieces on a microwave roasting rack or in a suitable shallow dish if a rack is not available. Squeeze

the lemon juice over and sprinkle with the mixed herbs. Cover.

2. Microwave on 100%/FULL power for 8–9 minutes, turning the chicken pieces over and re-covering once, half-way through. Set aside.

3. Put the onion, celery and pepper into a 2.3–2.8 litre (4–5 pint) casserole. Cover with a lid and microwave on 100%/FULL power for 3 minutes.

4. Stir in the rice. Drain the juices from the chicken into a measuring jug. Make the liquid up to 550ml (1 pint) with boiling stock. Pour on to the rice. Add the wine.

5. Cover and microwave on 100%/FULL power for 16–17 minutes then set aside, without removing the lid, for 10 minutes.

6. Stir the sweetcorn and peas into the rice after its standing time.

7. Remove the chicken from the bone and roughly chop. Fork into the rice mixture with the chopped tomatoes.

8. Cover and microwave on 100%/FULL power for 5 minutes.

9. Serve immediately, sprinkled with the parsley.

* A meal in itself, but you could serve a tossed green salad to accompany the risotto.

TOMATO CHICKEN DRUMSTICKS

Tomatoes are a good source of vitamins A and C, although some vitamin C is lost in the cooking. Skinned chicken drumsticks provide protein in this extremely colourful dish that is full of flavour. Popular for late-summer entertaining.

PREPARATION TIME (after assembling ingredients):
   10 minutes
MICROWAVE COOKING TIME: 22–5 minutes
SERVES: 4

900g (2lb) chicken drumsticks,   1 medium onion, finely
   skinned   chopped

1 clove garlic, chopped
1 × 400g (1 × 4oz) can chopped
  tomatoes
2 × 15ml spoon (2 tablespoons)
  tomato purée
freshly ground black pepper
a sprig of fresh marjoram

2 × 5ml spoons (2 teaspoons)
  cornflour, rounded

TO SERVE
plenty of freshly chopped
parsley

1. Put the chicken drumsticks into a 2.3 litre (4 pint) casserole dish. Add the onion with the tomatoes, tomato purée, garlic and black pepper. Stir gently to distribute evenly. Add the sprig of marjoram.

2. Cover with a lid and microwave on 100%/FULL power for 10 minutes. Stir to rearrange the chicken.

3. Re-cover and microwave on 100%/FULL power for 10–12 minutes, or until the chicken is tender. Set aside, covered, for 5 minutes, then lift the chicken drumsticks on to a warmed serving dish. Keep warm. Remove and discard the marjoram.

4. Blend the cornflour with a little water and add to the tomato mixture. Stir well.

5. Microwave, uncovered, on 100%/FULL power for 2–3 minutes, stirring frequently.

6. Pour the hot sauce over the drumsticks. Sprinkle with parsley and serve immediately with mashed potatoes and peas.

* To defrost 900g (2lb) frozen chicken drumsticks will take approximately 14 minutes using your DEFROST control. Rearrange the drumsticks twice during this time and allow to stand for 15 minutes before using.

* I suggest cooking the potatoes conventionally, with the minimum of water. Drain and mash with semi-skimmed milk. The peas may be microwaved during the standing time of the chicken – see point 3 (cover after cooking and they will keep hot while you complete the tomato sauce).

TURKEY MEDALLIONS WITH ORANGE SAUCE

No fat is used during the preparation of this recipe that provides a delicious main course suitable for entertaining. The lean turkey breast fillets provide protein and the breadcrumbs and almonds add fibre to the stuffing, which is lightly flavoured with orange juice and lemon rind.

PREPARATION TIME (after assembling ingredients): 25 minutes

MICROWAVE COOKING TIME: 19½–21 minutes

SERVES: 4

4 turkey breast fillets, about 150g (6oz) each

FOR THE STUFFING
50g (2oz) fresh brown breadcrumbs
25g (1oz) flaked almonds
1 small onion, finely chopped
25g (1oz) raisins
grated rind of ½ a lemon
3–4 × 15ml spoons (3–4 tablespoons) pure orange juice

FOR THE GLAZE
1 × 15ml spoon (1 tablespoon) set honey, level
2 × 15ml spoons (2 tablespoons) pure orange juice
pinch allspice
2 × 5ml spoons (2 teaspoons) arrowroot, level
chicken stock

TO SERVE
snipped chives, watercress

1. Put the turkey breasts, individually, between sheets of greaseproof paper and beat out until about 6mm (¼in) thick.
2. Prepare the stuffing: Put the breadcrumbs, almonds, raisins, onion, lemon rind and orange juice into a bowl. Mix to combine.
3. Divide equally between the turkey breasts and spread over.
4. Roll up and arrange the turkey breasts, close together, in a suitable fairly shallow dish.
5. Prepare the glaze: Put the honey, orange juice and allspice into a mug. Microwave, uncovered, on 100%/FULL power for 30–45 seconds. Stir.
6. Pour the glaze over the turkey breasts.

7. Cover and microwave on 100%/FULL power for 3 minutes, then baste with the glaze, re-cover and continue to microwave on 50%/MEDIUM for about 15 minutes, or until the turkey is opaque.
8. Allow to stand, covered, for 5 minutes, then drain off the liquid into a measuring jug. Make it up to 230ml (8fl oz) with the chicken stock.
9. Cream the arrowroot to a paste with a little water.
10. Stir into the liquid in the jug. Microwave, uncovered, on 100%/FULL power for 1–2 minutes, or until boiling and thickened. Stir frequently.
11. To serve: Carefully lift each turkey breast on to a chopping board. Cut into 3 even, thick slices.
12. Arrange the slices in a flan dish, flat, so that the filling is visible.
13. Pour over the sauce. Sprinkle with chives and serve with a watercress garnish, new potatoes and broccoli. Cook the vegetables conventionally in a minimum of water with a tightly fitting lid.

LIVER WITH MUSHROOMS

Protein, vitamin A and the B complex of vitamins are found in liver as well as an appreciable amount of iron. The mushrooms add fibre and a delicious flavour to this nutritious supper dish.

PREPARATION TIME (after assembling ingredients):
   20 minutes
MICROWAVE COOKING TIME: 8–9 minutes
SERVES: 4

550g (1¼lb) lambs liver
1½ × 15ml spoons (1½ rounded tablespoons) wholewheat flour seasoned with freshly ground black pepper and a little dried mixed herbs

2 × 15ml spoons (2 tablespoons) corn oil
225g (8oz) mushrooms, wiped and sliced
1 medium onion, chopped

1. Pre-heat a large, deep browning dish without the lid for 7 minutes on 100%/FULL power.
2. Cut the liver into thin strips 5mm (¼in) wide and toss in the seasoned flour.
3. Put 1 × 15ml spoon (1 tablespoon) oil into the hot dish with the mushrooms and onion. Stir until the dish stops sizzling.
4. Cover with the lid and microwave on 100%/FULL power for 3 minutes. Stir. Transfer to another dish with any liquid.
5. Reheat the browning dish, without the lid, for 2 minutes on 100%/FULL power.
6. Add the remaining oil, swirling it round the dish.
7. Add the floured liver, stirring and turning to seal all sides.
8. Cover with the lid and microwave on 100%/FULL power for 4 minutes. Stir. Stir in the mushrooms and onions with their liquid.
9. Cover and microwave on 100%/FULL power for 1–2 minutes to reheat. Stir.
10. Serve immediately with jacket potatoes and peas.

* Cook the jacket potatoes before the liver. Wrap them in clean towels and set aside. They will be quite hot enough to serve without reheating. The peas should be cooked after point 8 of the method and the liver reheated just before serving for 1–2 minutes on 100%/FULL power.

* A mustard sauce would go well with the liver and should be cooked conventionally. Use the roux method with semi-skimmed milk and a Dijon mustard.

CURRIED LIVER CASSEROLE

The microwave makes delicious casseroles and here a light curry powder is used to give an Eastern flavour to the pigs liver, which is high in protein, rich in vitamin A and the B complex vitamins, and a valuable source of iron. A lovely moist lunch or supper dish.

PREPARATION TIME (after assembling ingredients):
    15 minutes

MICROWAVE COOKING TIME: 25 minutes
SERVES: 4

450g (1lb) pigs liver
1 × 15ml spoon
   (1 tablespoon)
   wholewheat
   flour, level   mixed
1 × 15ml spoon   together
   (1 tablespoon)
   mild curry
   powder, level
2 medium onions, chopped
1 green pepper, deseeded and
   chopped

1 × 15ml spoon (1 tablespoon)
   corn oil
1 × 5ml spoon (1 teaspoon)
   dried marjoram *or* 2 sprigs
   of fresh marjoram
115ml (4fl oz) well-flavoured
   vegetable or beef stock,
   warm
freshly ground black pepper

1. Slice the liver into 4cm (1½in) wide slices and toss in the mixed curry powder and flour.
2. Put the oil into a casserole and microwave on 100%/FULL power for 1 minute. Stir in the onions and the green pepper.
3. Cover and microwave on 100%/FULL power for 3 minutes.
4. Stir in the liver. Cover and microwave on 100%/FULL power for 4 minutes.
5. Gently stir in the stock with the herbs and black pepper.
6. Cover and microwave on 100%/FULL power for 2 minutes, then continue to microwave on 40%/SIMMER for 15 minutes, or until the liver is tender. Stir and re-cover after 7 minutes.
7. Allow to stand for 5 minutes, then serve with boiled brown rice and the Broad Bean and Carrot Salad on p. 76.

*   Microwave the rice (see p. 80) before the liver dish is cooked and set aside, covered. It may be necessary to reheat this dish for 1–2 minutes, covered, while the liver has its final standing time. The Broad Bean and Carrot Salad may be prepared well in advance.

CHEESE-STUFFED MARROW

Nuts and cheese mixed with wholemeal breadcrumbs and herbs ring a pleasant change to the traditional stuffed marrow. Nuts and cheese both provide protein and Cheddar cheese is used here for its rich flavour.

PREPARATION TIME (after assembling ingredients):
10 minutes
MICROWAVE COOKING TIME: 18 minutes
SERVES: 4

FOR THE STUFFING
1 marrow, about 1kg (2¼lb)
1 medium onion, chopped
100g (4oz) cashew nuts, chopped
50g (2oz) wholemeal breadcrumbs
100g (4oz) Cheddar cheese, grated
1 × 5ml spoon (1 teaspoon) dill seeds

1 × 15ml spoon (1 tablespoon) tomato purée
freshly ground black pepper
1 egg, size 3, beaten
1 × 15ml spoon (1 tablespoon) semi-skimmed milk

TO GARNISH
75g (3oz) medium-sized button mushrooms
olive oil for brushing

1. Wipe the marrow clean and cut into 4cm (1½in) slices.
2. Remove the seeds, then arrange the slices, in a single layer, in a shallow dish.
3. Cover and microwave on 100%/FULL power for 6 minutes. Drain off the excess water.
4. Prepare the stuffing: Put the onion into a medium-sized bowl and microwave, uncovered, on 100%/FULL power for 2 minutes.
5. Add the chopped cashew nuts, breadcrumbs, Cheddar cheese, dill seeds and tomato purée. Season with the pepper. Remove the mushroom stalks, chop and add to the filling.
6. Beat the egg and milk together and use to bind the stuffing.
7. Divide the filling evenly between the part-cooked marrow slices.
8. Top each marrow slice with a button mushroom. Brush the mushrooms with the oil.
9. Cover and microwave on 100%/FULL power for about 10 minutes, or until the marrow is tender.

10. Allow to stand for 5 minutes, then serve with the Tomato Sauce on p. 45, which should be reheated for about 2 minutes on 100%/FULL power and stirred before serving.

* A pasta or rice salad would go well with this dish and could be prepared well in advance.

KIDNEYS IN MUSHROOM SAUCE

Rich in iron and vitamin A, kidneys remain full of flavour cooked the microwave way. High in protein, this recipe is quick to prepare and a good standby as kidneys freeze well and may be defrosted quickly in the microwave.

PREPARATION TIME (after assembling ingredients):
25 minutes
MICROWAVE COOKING TIME: 10–11 minutes
SERVES: 4

25g (1oz) polyunsaturated margarine
12 lambs kidneys, halved and cored
2 × 15ml spoons (2 tablespoons) wholemeal flour, seasoned with freshly ground black pepper

100g (4oz) mushrooms, finely chopped
140ml (¼ pint) semi-skimmed milk

TO SERVE
freshly chopped parsley

1. Put the margarine into a 1.7 litre (3 pint) casserole and microwave on 100%/FULL power for about 45 seconds or until melted.
2. Toss the kidneys in the seasoned flour and add to the hot margarine. Stir.
3. Cover and microwave on 100%/FULL power for 7 minutes.
4. Stir in the mushrooms and the milk. Season with a little black pepper.
5. Microwave, uncovered, on 100%/FULL power for 2–3 minutes, stirring every minute, or until the sauce boils and thickens.

6. Serve immediately, sprinkled with parsley and accompanied by Rice Medley (see p. 80).

* Prepare the rice dish first and set aside to stand while cooking the kidneys. It may need reheating, covered, for 1–2 minutes just before serving.

* To defrost 12 lambs kidneys will take 7 minutes using your DE-FROST control. Turn the kidneys over half-way through. Allow to stand for 15 minutes before using in this recipe.

* There is a fairly noticeable 'popping' sound while the kidneys are cooking – don't worry about it as it is a fairly common feature of microwave cooking.

TAGLIATELLE PORK

A good source of protein and vitamin B1, pork has a delicious flavour and the leg fillet used here provides a tender cut which is cooked on low power so that the flavours of the apricots and apple juice mingle well. Dried apricots are one of the best sources of dietary fibre. They also give colour to the dish.

PREPARATION TIME (after assembling ingredients):
15–20 minutes
MICROWAVE COOKING TIME:
48 minutes (for both pasta and pork)
SERVES: 6

1 medium onion, peeled and ringed	2 medium tomatoes, peeled and chopped
1 × 15ml spoon (1 tablespoon) wholemeal flour, level	115ml (4fl oz) apple juice freshly ground black pepper
1 medium red pepper, deseeded and thinly sliced	sprig of fresh thyme 350g (12oz) tagliatelle verde
100g (4oz) dried apricots	1 × 5ml spoon (1 teaspoon)
450g (1lb) pork fillet, diced	olive oil

1. Cook the pork sauce: Put the onion into a 1.7 litre (3 pint) casserole dish and microwave, covered, on 100%/FULL power for 2 minutes.
2. Sprinkle over the flour, then add the red pepper, dried

117

apricots, pork fillet and chopped tomatoes. Pour over the apple juice. Season with black pepper. Lay the thyme on top.

3. Cover and microwave on 100%/FULL power for 6 minutes, then gently stir and continue to microwave on 40%/SIMMER for 30 minutes, or until the pork is tender. Set aside, covered.

4. Cook the tagliatelle: Put the pasta into a 2.3–2.8 litre (4–5 pint) casserole. Pour over a kettle of boiling water.

5. Add the oil. Cover and microwave on 100%/FULL power for 10 minutes, stirring and re-covering once using the handle of a wooden spoon half-way through cooking.

6. Set aside, covered, for 5 minutes, then drain and quickly rinse with plenty of boiling water.

7. Arrange on a serving dish and serve immediately topped with the sauce (discard the thyme).

* A tomato and watercress salad would be an excellent accompaniment to the Tagliatelle Pork.

BEEF AND KIDNEY CASSEROLE

Kidney beans, high in fibre and containing protein, are used here to extend the lean beef and lambs kidneys, which are rich in iron and also provide vitamin A. The casserole is a meal in itself, ideal for a winter's evening.

PREPARATION TIME (after assembling ingredients): 20 minutes

MICROWAVE COOKING TIME: 1 hour 33 minutes (for both the beans and the casserole) + grilling time

SERVES: 4

50g (2oz) red kidney beans, soaked overnight
275g (10oz) chuck steak, cubed, all visible fat removed
4 lambs kidneys, skinned, halved and cored

1 × 15ml spoon (1 tablespoon) wholewheat flour, rounded
1 × 15ml spoon (1 tablespoon) corn oil
1 × 150g (6oz) potato, washed and diced
2 medium onions, ringed

1 green pepper, deseeded and
  sliced
2 cloves garlic, crushed
1 × 397g (14oz) can chopped
  tomatoes
140ml (¼ pint) good beef
  stock, warm
1 × 5ml spoon (1 teaspoon)
  dried basil

TO SERVE
2 fairly thick slices from a
  wholemeal loaf, cubed
plenty of freshly chopped
  parsley

1. Cook the soaked kidney beans: Drain and rinse the soaked
   beans, then put them into a 2.3 litre (4 pint) casserole dish.
   Cover with boiling water. Cover with a lid and microwave
   on 100%/FULL power for 20 minutes. Set aside to stand.

2. Toss the chuck steak and the prepared kidneys in the flour
   (this is easiest done in a polythene bag).

3. Put the oil into a 1.7–2.3 litre (3–4 pint) casserole and
   microwave, uncovered, on 100%/FULL power for 1 minute.

4. Stir in the potato, onion, green pepper and the tossed meats.
   Cover and microwave on 100%/FULL power for 6 minutes.

5. Add the garlic with the chopped tomatoes and the stock,
   then add the basil. Stir well.

6. Cover and microwave on 100%/FULL power for 6 minutes.
   Carefully lift the lid and stir in the drained kidney beans.

7. Cover and microwave on DEFROST for 1 hour. Stir and
   re-cover three times during cooking. Set aside, covered, for
   15 minutes, then prepare the topping.

8. Cube the bread, then toast under a pre-heated grill on one
   side only. I find it easiest to do this if the bread is arranged
   on a fireproof plate.

9. Using oven gloves, scoop the toasted bread on to the cooked
   casserole. Sprinkle with the chopped parsley and serve
   immediately with a coleslaw salad.

CHEESE SCONE PIZZA

Stacked high with its low-fat topping, this high-fibre pizza will
soon become a firm favourite with all the family. I like to pop it

under a pre-heated grill for 2 or 3 minutes after microwaving to give the cheese a golden tinge. Very easy to prepare and cook.

PREPARATION TIME (after assembling ingredients):
   30 minutes
MICROWAVE COOKING TIME: 16–17 minutes
SERVES: 4–6

FOR THE SCONE BASE
150g (6oz) self-raising wholewheat flour
½ × 5ml spoon (½ teaspoon) baking powder
40g (1½oz) polyunsaturated margarine, chilled
50g (2oz) Shape low-fat Cheddar cheese, grated
½ × 5ml spoon (1 teaspoon) dried oregano
1 egg, size 3, beaten with about 4 × 15ml spoons (4 tablespoons) semi-skimmed milk

FOR THE TOPPING
1 medium onion, chopped
1 medium green pepper, chopped
1 courgette, sliced
1 × 400g (14oz) can chopped tomatoes
100g (4oz) button mushrooms, sliced
2 × 15ml spoons (2 tablespoons) tomato purée
1 clove garlic, crushed
freshly ground black pepper
100g (4oz) Edam cheese, grated

1. Prepare the topping: Put the onion, green pepper and courgette into a medium-sized casserole. Cover with a lid.
2. Microwave on 100%/FULL power for 4 minutes. Stir.
3. Put the tomatoes in a sieve to drain off excess moisture. Use this liquid in another recipe.
4. Stir the mushrooms, drained tomatoes and tomato purée into the casserole with the garlic. Season with black pepper.
5. Microwave, uncovered, on 100%/FULL power for 5 minutes, stirring after 3 minutes. Stir and set aside.
6. Make the scone base: Put the flour and baking powder into a mixing bowl. Rub in the margarine until the mixture resembles fine breadcrumbs.
7. Mix in the grated cheese with the oregano.
8. Add the egg and milk and mix to form a soft dough.
9. Knead lightly, using a little extra wholemeal flour if

necessary. Roll out to a circle to fit a 23cm (9in) dinner-plate. Lift on to the plate.

10. Pinch the edge, all the way round, between your thumb and first finger to form a pattern.

11. Microwave, uncovered, on 100%/FULL power for 4 minutes.

12. Spread the prepared filling evenly over the base.

13. Cover evenly with the grated Edam cheese.

14. Return to the microwave, uncovered, on 100%/FULL power for 3–4 minutes or until the cheese has melted.

15. Serve hot or warm with coleslaw salad.

* To reheat a slice of this pizza will take 1½–2 minutes, uncovered, on 100%/FULL power.

ROAST DUCK WITH GRAPEFRUIT SAUCE

Duck contains more fat than turkey or chicken but, cooked as directed here, the fat will drain away and a delicious crisp roast duckling will result which is not at all fatty. As there is little meat on the bones, allow 350g (12oz) uncooked duck per person. The grapefruit sauce provides a tangy change from the traditional orange, cherry or apple sauce.

PREPARATION TIME (after assembling ingredients):
   10 minutes
MICROWAVE COOKING TIME: about 43–4 minutes
SERVES: 3

1 roasting duck, 1.85kg (4lb 2oz) fully defrosted, if frozen
1 × 15ml spoon (1 tablespoon) soya sauce
1 × 15ml spoon (1 tablespoon) water
2 × 5ml spoon (2 teaspoons) honey, level

150ml (¼ pint) dry white wine
150ml (¼ pint) duck stock, made from the giblets
2 × 5ml spoons (2 teaspoons) honey, level
1 × 15ml spoon (1 tablespoon) cornflour, rounded
freshly ground black pepper

FOR THE SAUCE
2 grapefruits

1. Remove the giblets and use to make the stock.
2. Wipe the duck all over with absorbent kitchen paper or a clean tea-towel to dry it thoroughly.
3. Prick the skin on all sides with a skewer so that the fat will run out freely.
4. Put the soya sauce, water and honey into a mug and microwave on 100%/FULL power for about 45 seconds, or until warm.
5. Lift the dried duck, breast side down, on to a microwave roasting rack and, using a pastry brush, brush all over with the soya sauce and honey mixture.
6. Cover with a split roasting bag and microwave on 100%/FULL power for 20 minutes. Remove from the oven and allow to stand for 15 minutes. Pour off the fat and juices.
7. Carefully turn the duck over and shield the wings by wrapping them in thin strips of foil.
8. Brush the breast with any remaining soya sauce and honey mixture. Cover again with the split roasting bag and microwave on 100%/FULL power for 17 minutes.
9. Remove from the microwave. Pour off the fat and juices again. Cover with a tent of foil and set aside for 15 minutes.
10. Meanwhile pre-heat the *conventional* oven to 400°F, gas mark 6, 200°C.
11. Prepare the sauce: Put the grated rind and the juice of 1 grapefruit into a 1 litre jug with the wine, duck stock and the honey. Season with a little black pepper. Microwave on 100%/FULL power for 3 minutes.
12. Mix the cornflour to a smooth paste with a little water in a 1.7 litre (3 pint) mixing bowl. Pour on the heated liquid, stirring continuously. Microwave, uncovered, on 100%/FULL power for 2–3 minutes, or until thickened and boiling, stirring frequently.
13. Lift the duck on to an ovenproof dish (leave the foil in place). Put into the pre-heated oven and roast uncovered for about 15 minutes, or until crisp and brown. As more fat runs out, baste the breast.
14. Segment the remaining grapefruit, discarding all pith and skin, and add to the sauce.

15. Place the browned duck on to a warmed serving dish. Surround it with a selection of lightly cooked vegetables and serve the grapefruit sauce separately.

CURRIED VEGETABLES WITH EGG

A tasty high-fibre, low-calorie meal which is economical to make. Hard-boiled eggs give protein and colour to the dish. Remember that eggs should not be boiled in the microwave oven as the pressure builds up under the shell and they may explode.

PREPARATION TIME (after assembling ingredients):
    12 minutes
MICROWAVE COOKING TIME: about 2½–3 minutes
SERVES: 4

450g (1lb) leeks, cleaned and sliced
1 medium aubergine, diced, salted and rinsed (see note)
1 medium green pepper, chopped
40g (1½oz) polyunsaturated margarine

40g (1½oz) wholewheat flour
1 × 15ml spoon (1 tablespoon) mild curry powder, level
425ml (16fl oz) semi-skimmed milk or chicken stock
100g (4oz) mushrooms, sliced
4 eggs, size 3, hard-boiled then plunged into cold water

1. Put the prepared leeks, aubergine and pepper into a 1.7 litre (3 pint) casserole dish. Add 3 × 15ml spoons (3 tablespoons) water.
2. Cover and microwave on 100%/FULL power for 15 minutes, stirring and re-covering after 7 minutes. Set aside, covered.
3. Put the margarine into a 1 litre jug and microwave on 100%/FULL power for about 45 seconds or until melted and hot.
4. Stir in the flour and curry powder. Add the milk or stock, carefully blending in the first drop of milk, then pouring in the remainder, stirring.
5. Microwave, uncovered, on 100%/FULL power for 4–5

minutes. Beat well with a balloon whisk after 2 minutes and again at the end of the cooking time.

6. Add the mushrooms to the cooked vegetables, gently stirring them into the liquid the vegetables have produced.

7. Shell the eggs and quarter them lengthways. Arrange on the vegetables.

8. Pour the curry sauce over to coat.

9. Cover and microwave on 100%/FULL power for 1–2 minutes to reheat.

10. Serve immediately with cooked rice or wholemeal bread or scones.

* To remove the bitter taste from the aubergines they should be put into a colander, sprinkled liberally with salt, then set aside for 15 minutes, topped with a side-plate and a weight of some kind. Rinse well under cold running water before using in the recipe.

CHICK PEA CASSEROLE

The apple juice, chilli, garlic, tomato purée and curry powder give the chick peas and vegetables a delicious flavour. Chick peas add protein and fibre to this main meal dish.

PREPARATION TIME (after assembling ingredients):
20 minutes
MICROWAVE COOKING TIME: 1 hour 5 minutes
SERVES: 4

225g (8oz) dried chick peas, soaked overnight in cold water
450g (1lb) potatoes, scrubbed clean and roughly chopped
450g (1lb) carrots, peeled and diced
2 leeks, sliced, or 1 large onion, chopped
140ml (¼ pint) apple juice

1 green chilli, seeds discarded, chopped
2 cloves garlic, crushed
2 × 5ml spoons (2 teaspoons) mild curry powder
2 × 15ml spoons (2 tablespoons) tomato purée
140ml (¼ pint) well-flavoured chicken stock, cold

1. Cook the chick peas: Drain the soaked chick peas and put into a 2.3 litre (4 pint) casserole dish.
2. Cover with boiling water. Top with a lid and microwave on 100%/FULL power for 10 minutes. Then continue to microwave, covered, on 40%/SIMMER for 30 minutes, or until tender. Set aside for 5 minutes, then drain.
3. Put the potatoes and carrots, and the leeks or onion, into a 2.3 litre (4 pint) casserole dish.
4. Mix together the apple juice, chopped chilli, garlic, curry powder and tomato purée. Add to the casserole.
5. Cover with a lid and microwave on 100%/FULL power for 10 minutes. Stir in the chick peas and stock.
6. Cover and microwave on 100%/FULL power for 15 minutes.
7. Allow to stand, covered, for 5 minutes before serving with a mixed salad and bread.

VEAL ESCALOPES WITH MUSHROOM STUFFING

Veal, a high-protein food that is lower in calories than pork, beef or lamb, is flavoured with a delicious mushroom and orange stuffing. Serve with the Mushroom Sauce on p. 126, which should be made using the juices from the cooked veal (see recipe).

PREPARATION TIME (after assembling ingredients):
    12 minutes
MICROWAVE COOKING TIME: 10 minutes
SERVES: 4–6

4 veal escalopes, each
    weighing about 150g (6oz)
50g (2oz) mushrooms, finely
    chopped
grated rind of ½ an orange
2 shallots or pickling onions,
    chopped
25g (1oz) wholemeal
    breadcrumbs, fresh
½ × 5ml spoon (½ teaspoon)
    dried tarragon

freshly ground black pepper
a little beaten egg to bind
2 × 15ml spoons (2
    tablespoons) pure
    orange juice

TO GARNISH
wedges of fresh orange
sprigs of watercress

1. Lay the veal between two layers of dampened greaseproof paper and roll out with a rolling pin to flatten – I find it easier to do this individually.
2. Mix together the mushrooms, orange rind, chopped shallots or pickling onions, breadcrumbs and tarragon. Season with a little black pepper.
3. Add a little beaten egg to bind the ingredients together.
4. Divide the filling evenly between the escalopes, spreading it all over, but not quite up to the edge.
5. Roll up each escalope and lift into a shallow, round dish. They should be close together and supporting each other, but if preferred secure with *wooden* cocktail sticks to prevent unrolling. Pour the orange juice over.
6. Cover and microwave on 70%/ROAST for 10 minutes. Allow to stand, covered, for 7 minutes.
7. Slice each veal roll into four fairly thick slices, and arrange so that the stuffing is visible, flat, on a serving dish.
8. Prepare the sauce (see below) and pour over to coat.
9. Garnish with wedges of orange and sprigs of watercress and serve immediately with courgettes, which may be cooked during the standing time of the veal.

*   As an alternative serve the veal topped with the Mushroom Sauce and sprinkled with a topping made from dried, crushed breadcrumbs and grated half-fat Cheddar cheese. (The bread should be dried out in your conventional oven and then 'crumbed' with a rolling pin.)

MUSHROOM SAUCE

Semi-skimmed milk adds protein but little fat to this sauce, which has a delicious flavour from the veal juices and the orange in the previous recipe. Mushrooms add taste and fibre. If not serving with the veal dish, use semi-skimmed milk or vegetable stock for the total amount of liquid.

PREPARATION TIME (after assembling ingredients):
5 minutes

MICROWAVE COOKING TIME: 2–3 minutes (depending on
   starting temperature of the liquid – see method)
SERVES: 4

285ml (½ pint) liquid – stock,
   semi-skimmed milk or
   cooking juices from the veal
   recipe made up with milk

15g (½oz) cornflour
75g (3oz) button mushrooms,
   finely chopped

1. In a 1.1 litre (2 pint) jug, or in a large bowl, blend the
    cornflour with a little cold milk. Stir in the remaining
    liquid.
2. Microwave, uncovered, on 100%/FULL power for 2–3 min-
    utes, stirring frequently, or until boiling and thickened.
3. Stir in the mushrooms, which will cook quite sufficiently in
    the heat of the sauce. Use as required.

PICNIC LOAF

Bulgar wheat is available in health food shops. It is very simple
to use and in this recipe it extends the meat to produce a meat
loaf which is high in protein and vitamins.

PREPARATION TIME (after assembling ingredients):
   7 minutes + soaking time
MICROWAVE COOKING TIME: 15 minutes
SERVES: 4

40g (1½oz) bulgar wheat
1 onion, finely chopped
200g (8oz) raw minced, lean
   pork
225g (8oz) raw chicken livers,
   membranes discarded,
   chopped
2 × 15ml spoons (2
   tablespoons) red wine or
   beef stock

½ × 5ml spoon (½ teaspoon)
   dried rosemary
freshly ground black pepper
1 carrot, peeled and grated
2 × 15ml spoons (2
   tablespoons) soya sauce

1. Put the bulgar wheat into a medium bowl. Cover with cold
    water and leave to soak for 15–20 minutes.

2. Drain through a sieve, pressing out excess water with a wooden spoon. Turn into a large bowl.
3. Add all the remaining ingredients to the bulgar wheat and mix well.
4. Turn into a 1.7 litre (3 pint) microwave bread-baker and level the top.
5. Stand on a plate.
6. Cover and microwave on 70%/ROAST for 15 minutes.
7. Allow to cool in container, then turn out and serve, sliced, with a mixed salad.

SPICED LAMB WITH MUSHROOMS

The lamb is marinaded in a spicy mixture before cooking. The resulting dish is beautifully tender and has an Eastern flavour. Lamb is a high-protein food and leg of lamb is a particularly lean cut. Mushrooms add fibre to the dish.

PREPARATION TIME (after assembling ingredients):
    10 minutes + time for marinading
MICROWAVE COOKING TIME: 15–17 minutes
SERVES: 4

1 × 15ml spoon (1 tablespoon) corn oil
450g (1lb) leg of lamb, fat and bone removed, cubed
100g (4oz) mushrooms, sliced
225ml (8fl oz) warm stock, lamb or vegetable
1 × 15ml spoon (1 tablespoon) cornflour, level

FOR THE MARINADE
2 × 15ml spoons (2 tablespoons) pure orange juice

1 × 15ml spoon (1 tablespoon) tomato purée
2 × 15ml spoons (2 tablespoons) corn oil
1 clove garlic, crushed
1 × 5ml spoon (1 teaspoon) ground coriander
1 × 5ml spoon (1 teaspoon) turmeric
freshly ground black pepper

1. Put the cubed lamb into a shallow dish.
2. Mix together all the ingredients for the marinade, until

blended. Pour over the meat. Turn the meat in the marinade so that flavours will penetrate, then cover and set aside for at least 2 hours.

3. Pre-heat a large deep browning dish, without its lid, for 7 minutes on 100%/FULL power.

4. Put the oil into the heated dish. Swirl it round to heat, then carefully add the lamb with most of the marinade, pressing and turning it on the hot dish until the sizzling stops.

5. Cover and microwave on 100%/FULL power for 4–6 minutes, stirring after 2 minutes.

6. Blend the cornflour with a little cold water in a large bowl.

7. Add the warm stock to the blended cornflour, mixing well.

8. Add the mushrooms with the cornflour and stock mixture to the browning dish.

9. Microwave, uncovered, on 100%/FULL power for 4 minutes, stirring frequently.

10. Allow to stand, covered, for 7 minutes, then serve with rice or jacket potatoes and cauliflower.

* The rice or potatoes may be microwaved before the lamb is cooked. Set aside, covered, they will keep their heat while the lamb cooks. To save time the cauliflower should be cooked conventionally in the minimum of water.

BRAISED CHICKEN WITH PEANUT SAUCE

A little butter is used in the sauce of this dish for its superb flavour. A healthy, low-fat, special meal. Serve with jacket potatoes and Brussels sprouts.

PREPARATION TIME (after assembling ingredients):
    15 minutes
MICROWAVE COOKING TIME: about 49–55 minutes
SERVES: 4–6

1 × 1.8kg (4lb) roasting
  chicken, free-range if
  possible
½ a lemon
1 onion, peeled and sliced

1 stick celery, chopped
1 carrot, peeled and sliced
140ml (¼ pint) chicken stock
small bunch fresh herbs, tied
  together

6 black peppercorns

FOR THE SAUCE
30g (1¼oz) butter
30g (1¼oz) wholewheat flour
liquid from chicken, made up
 to 340ml (12fl oz) with water,
 if necessary

2 × 15ml spoons (2
tablespoons) smooth peanut
butter, level

TO SERVE
wedges of fresh orange
sprigs of fresh parsley

1. Remove the giblets from the chicken. Rub the bird all over with the cut lemon half, then put the lemon into the body cavity. Tie the legs together with string.
2. Arrange the prepared vegetables in the base of a large casserole dish. Add the giblets, the bunch of herbs and the peppercorns.
3. Sit the prepared chicken on the vegetables and pour over the stock. Cover with a lid.
4. Microwave on 70%/ROAST for 45–50 minutes, or until the chicken is tender – test by inserting a sharp knife between thigh and breast and make sure that juices run clear. Any pink juices indicate that the chicken is not cooked. Cover and return to the microwave for 5 minutes. Test again.
5. Set aside, covered, for 10 minutes.
6. Remove the chicken and lift on to a warmed serving dish. Cover and keep warm.
7. Strain the liquid from the chicken and measure. Make it up to 340ml (12fl oz) with water, if necessary.
8. Put the butter into a large bowl. Microwave, uncovered, on 100%/FULL power for 45 seconds or until melted and hot. Stir in the flour, blending well.
9. Gradually add the stock, stirring.
10. Microwave, uncovered, on 100%/FULL power for 3–4 minutes, beating well with a balloon whisk every minute.
11. Stir in the peanut butter.

* The potatoes should be microwaved before the chicken is cooked. Wrap individually in foil, shiny side inside, and set aside. They will hold their heat for 45 minutes. Just before serving, remove the foil and microwave them all together for 2 minutes on 100%/FULL power. The sprouts should be cooked conventionally for this meal.

12. To serve, carve the chicken into joints and arrange on a serving dish. Pour the sauce over to coat. Garnish with the orange wedges and parsley sprigs and serve with the jacket potatoes and Brussels sprouts.

VEGETARIAN SUPPER DISH

Brown rice and red kidney beans are both high-fibre foods. The courgettes will give the rice a creamy taste and their vivid colour is an attractive addition. The toasted nut garnish provides protein, and of course flavour, in this vegetarian recipe.

PREPARATION TIME (after assembling ingredients):
  12 minutes
MICROWAVE COOKING TIME: about 1 hour
SERVES: 4

225g (8oz) red kidney beans, soaked overnight
1 clove garlic, crushed
1 medium onion, peeled and chopped
2 × 5ml spoons (2 teaspoons) olive oil
450g (1lb) courgettes, sliced

225g (8oz) Uncle Ben's wholegrain rice
550ml (1 pint) vegetable stock, boiling
1 wine glass apple juice
100g (4oz) vegetarian cheese, cubed
75g (3oz) toasted cashew nuts

1. Put the *drained* red kidney beans into a 2.3 litre (4 pint) casserole dish. Cover with boiling water.
2. Cover with a lid and microwave on 100%/FULL power for 10 minutes, then continue to microwave on 40%/SIMMER for 20–25 minutes, or until the beans are tender. Set aside for 5 minutes, then drain and keep covered.
3. Put the garlic, onion and the oil into a 2.3–2.7 litre (4–5 pint) casserole. Cover with a lid and microwave on 100%/FULL power for 2 minutes.
4. Stir in the courgettes, cover and microwave on 100%/FULL power for 3 minutes. Stir in the rice and pour over the boiling stock. Add the apple juice.

5. Cover and microwave on 100%/FULL power for 20 minutes.
6. Set aside, without removing lid, for 10 minutes, then fluff up the rice and add the drained kidney beans.
7. Cover and microwave on 100%/FULL power for 1–2 minutes to reheat. Fork in the cheese just before serving.
8. Serve immediately topped with the toasted cashew nuts and accompanied by a tossed green salad.

LENTILS WITH CHICKEN AND PEAS

Lentils are a useful source of protein and they also contain fibre, vitamin B6, iron and calcium. They are very filling, and this delicious main meal is made using the minimum of the more expensive ingredients. Chicken is high in protein and low in fat. Peas add fibre and some protein. They are also highly colourful.

PREPARATION TIME (after assembling ingredients):
   5 minutes
MICROWAVE COOKING TIME: 26 minutes
SERVES: 4

1 medium onion, chopped
2 rashers streaky bacon, de-rinded and chopped
225g (8oz) red split lentils, rinsed in cold water
100g (4oz) frozen peas

freshly ground black pepper
156g (6oz) cooked chicken meat
2 × 15ml spoons (2 tablespoons) grated Parmesan cheese

1. Put the onion and bacon into a 2.3 litre (4 pint) casserole. Cover and microwave on 100%/FULL power for 3 minutes.
2. Stir in the lentils and pour on 900ml (30fl oz) boiling water. Microwave, covered, on 70%/ROAST for about 20 minutes.
3. Allow to stand, covered, for 5 minutes, then stir in the frozen peas. Season with black pepper.
4. Cover and microwave on 100%/FULL power for 3 minutes, stirring and re-covering after 2 minutes.
5. Carefully stir in the cooked chicken.

6. Serve immediately sprinkled with plenty of grated Parmesan. A wholemeal French stick and a mixed salad would be ideal with this recipe.

RICE AND GRAINS JAMBOREE

Rice and grains is a blend of brown rice, whole oats, barley, wheat, rye, buckwheat and sesame seeds. It provides over 50% more protein per serving than rice alone, is low in fat, and is a rich source of dietary fibre. It is extremely versatile and has a lovely nutty flavour. Try this colourful dish hot or cold.

PREPARATION TIME (after assembling ingredients):
  10 minutes
MICROWAVE COOKING TIME: 38 minutes
SERVES: 4

1 medium onion, chopped
225g (8oz) Jordans country
  rice and grains
550ml (1 pint) chicken stock,
  hot
1 × 425g can pineapple pieces
  in natural juice, drained

75g (3oz) frozen peas
2 bacon steaks, all visible fat
  removed

TO SERVE
freshly chopped parsley

1. Put the onion into a 2.25 litre (4 pint) bowl. Cover and microwave on 100%/FULL power for 2 minutes. Stir in the rice and grains with the hot stock.
2. Cover and microwave on 100%/FULL power for 30 minutes.
3. Allow to stand, covered, for 10 minutes, then stir in the pineapple pieces and the frozen peas. Set aside.
4. Arrange the bacon chops on two sheets of absorbent kitchen paper on a dinner-plate. Cover with one sheet of absorbent kitchen paper.
5. Microwave on 70%/ROAST for 4 minutes. Set aside.
6. Pop the rice and grains back into the microwave, covered, on 100%/FULL power for 2 minutes to reheat, then turn on to a serving dish.

7. Cut the bacon into thin strips and arrange on the cooked rice and grains.
8. Sprinkle with parsley and serve immediately with a mixed salad or ratatouille.

CASHEW-STUFFED CHICKEN BREASTS

Lean, protein-packed chicken breasts with a delicious nutty stuffing – ideal for entertaining. Serve with rice or a selection of vegetables. The breasts are skinned as the skin harbours most of the fat found in chicken. Serve on a bed of freshly cooked pasta.

PREPARATION TIME (after assembling ingredients):
    15 minutes
MICROWAVE COOKING TIME: 15 minutes
SERVES: 4

4 chicken breasts, each weighing about 225g (8oz), skinned
4 × 15ml spoons (4 tablespoons) tomato juice

FOR THE STUFFING
1 medium onion, chopped
25g (1oz) cashew nuts, chopped
50g (2oz) wholemeal breadcrumbs

½ × 5ml spoon (½ teaspoon) dried mixed herbs
25g (1oz) raisins
freshly ground black pepper
a little semi-skimmed milk to bind

TO GARNISH
freshly chopped parsley

1. Prepare the stuffing: Put the onion into a medium bowl. Cover and microwave on 100%/FULL power for 3 minutes.
2. Stir in the cashew nuts, breadcrumbs, raisins and the mixed herbs. Season with a little pepper. Add sufficient milk to bind the ingredients together.
3. Cut a 'pocket' in the longer side of each chicken portion.
4. Divide the filling evenly between the chicken breast pockets.
5. Arrange the chicken breasts in ring fashion in a round

shallow dish. Pour 1 × 15ml (1 tablespoon) tomato juice over each one.

6. Cover and microwave on 100%/FULL power for 7 minutes. Turn each chicken piece over. Re-cover and microwave on 100%/FULL power for 5 minutes. Allow to stand, covered, for 5 minutes, then serve garnished with the chopped parsley.

DESSERTS

Healthy eating doesn't necessarily mean forgoing a pudding, although the easiest, most healthy dessert has always been a piece of fresh fruit.

People look forward to the finale of the meal, so I have used healthy ingredients, such as fruit, wholemeal flour and nuts, and combined them in different ways to make a variety of interesting dessert dishes. Serve a low-calorie ice cream or yoghurt instead of custard or cream to accompany the dessert where applicable and therefore reduce your intake of fat, which is very high in cream.

Sometimes sugar has to be used, so choose unrefined brown sugar instead of castor or granulated sugar, and serve smaller portions of desserts made with sugar, extending them with fresh fruit and yoghurt.

APPLE LAYER CRUNCH

A quick and easy combination of Bramley apples and a crunchy breakfast cereal. High in fibre and quick to cook, this dessert will be popular with nearly everyone.

PREPARATION TIME (after assembling ingredients):
   7 minutes
MICROWAVE COOKING TIME: 5–7 minutes
SERVES: 4

900g (2lb) Bramley cooking apples, peeled and sliced
3 × 15ml spoons (3 tablespoons) Lemon and Lime Curd (see p. 148)
1 × 15ml spoon (1 tablespoon) demerara sugar, level

150g (6oz) Jordans original crunchy toasted oat cereal with honey, almonds and raisins

136

1. Put the apples into a large mixing bowl or casserole with the Lemon and Lime Curd and the sugar. Add 1 × 15ml spoon (1 tablespoon) water.
2. Cover and microwave on 100%/FULL power for 5–7 minutes, or until the Bramleys are 'pulpy'. Stir and re-cover after 3 minutes.
3. Stir and set aside, covered, to cool.
4. Turn into a serving dish. Top with the crunchy cereal and serve immediately.

* Jordans cereal is prepared from entirely natural ingredients. It contains no artificial additives, colourings or preservatives. It is available from most supermarkets.

LEMON AND APPLE CHEESECAKE

Traditional cheesecake is high in fat and can be too heavy after a main course. Try this light, low-fat version that may be made a day in advance and stored in the refrigerator.

> PREPARATION TIME (after assembling ingredients):
>   20 minutes
> MICROWAVE COOKING TIME: 4–5 minutes
> SERVES: 6–8

grated rind and juice of 2 lemons
1 × 11g (0.4oz) sachet powdered gelatine
3 × 15ml spoons (3 tablespoons) cold water
10 digestive biscuits, crushed
50g (2oz) low-fat margarine spread
1 × 170g can evaporated milk
2 × 15ml spoons (2 tablespoons) concentrated apple juice, level

150g (6oz) quark (skimmed-milk soft cheese)
3 × 15ml spoons (3 tablespoons) soft light-brown sugar, level

TO DECORATE
1 green- or red-skinned eating apple
lemon juice

1. Put the lemons on to a plate and microwave on 100%/FULL power for 1 minute or until slightly warm.

2. Sprinkle the gelatine on to the water in a suitable bowl and set aside.

3. Put the low-fat margarine spread into a 1.7 litre (3 pint) mixing bowl and microwave on 40%/SIMMER for 1–2 minutes, or until melted.

4. Stir in the crushed biscuits. Stir well.

5. Turn into a loose-bottomed 20cm (8in) cake tin. Refrigerate.

6. Microwave the gelatine, uncovered, for about 2 minutes on 40%/SIMMER. Stir to ensure the gelatine has dissolved.

7. Meanwhile beat the evaporated milk with an electric mixer or with a rotary hand whisk until very thick.

8. Stir the lemon rind and juice into the dissolved gelatine with the apple concentrate.

9. Turn the mixer to a lower speed, if using one, and gradually beat in the gelatine mixture until combined. Continue to beat, gradually adding the cheese and sugar.

10. Turn on to the refrigerated biscuit base and return to the fridge until set firm.

11. To serve: Remove the cheesecake from the cake tin and place on a serving dish. Core and thinly slice the apple, but do not peel. Brush the apple slices on both sides with a little lemon juice to prevent discoloration and arrange them in an attractive pattern around the edge of the cheesecake.

* The digestive biscuits used for the base can easily be crushed in a food processor. Otherwise put them in a plastic bag and crush with a rolling pin.

FRUIT JELLY

A light and refreshing dessert using wholesome ingredients and no sugar. This well-flavoured jelly is ideal as a centrepiece on a buffet table. A low-calorie dessert.

PREPARATION TIME (after assembling ingredients):
   15 minutes
MICROWAVE COOKING TIME: 3–4 minutes
SERVES: 8

825ml (30fl oz) unsweetened
   red grape juice
2 × 5ml spoons (2 teaspoons)
   runny honey
1 banana, peeled and sliced
lemon juice
227g (8oz) can unsweetened
   pineapple pieces in natural
   juice, drained

2 × 11g (0.4oz) sachets
   powdered gelatine

TO SERVE
Greek yoghurt (optional)

1. Put 115ml (4fl oz) grape juice into a small bowl. Sprinkle over the gelatine and set aside for 15 minutes.

2. Meanwhile rinse a 1.7 litre (3 pint) reusable microwave soufflé dish with cold water.

3. Microwave the soaked gelatine, uncovered, for 3–4 minutes on 40%/SIMMER, stirring after 2 minutes. Stir to ensure the gelatine has dissolved. Stir in the honey to dissolve.

4. Stir into the remaining grape juice.

5. Pour a little of the prepared jelly into the soufflé dish – just enough to cover the base. Refrigerate until set.

6. Brush the banana slices with the lemon juice and arrange on the jelly layer.

7. Carefully cover with a layer of jelly. Refrigerate to set.

8. Arrange the drained pineapple slices over the set jelly.

9. Pour on the remaining liquid jelly and refrigerate until set firm.

10. When ready to serve, dip the mould in very hot water to come right up to the rim. Count to 7.

11. Turn out on to a serving dish and serve with Greek yoghurt.

* It is important to allow each layer to set completely before continuing.

* The canned pineapple must be drained and then dried on absorbent kitchen paper. As an alternative to the pineapple use 225g (8oz) fresh strawberries, hulled and halved.

NUTTY FRUIT CAKE

This high-fibre cake is delicious served as a dessert or as a tea-time treat. It will keep well in an airtight tin but do be careful not to overcook it. Cakes are cooked when the surface is just set. They continue to cook in their standing time. A good test to see if the cake is cooked is to insert a wooden cocktail stick into the centre – it should come out clean. Do this test after the standing time.

PREPARATION TIME (after assembling ingredients):
   10 minutes
MICROWAVE COOKING TIME: 8 minutes
SERVES: 4

100g (4oz) polyunsaturated
  margarine
75g (3oz) muscovado sugar
2 large eggs, beaten, size 2
1 × 5ml spoon (1 teaspoon)
  cinnamon, level
100g (4oz) self-raising
  wholewheat flour
50g (2oz) dried apricots,
  chopped

50g (2oz) roughly chopped
  dates
rind and juice of ½ an orange

TOPPING
50g (2oz) toasted flaked
  almonds

1. Lightly grease a 1.7 litre (3 pint) reusable microwave soufflé dish. Place a circle of greaseproof paper in the base, but do not grease the paper.
2. Beat the margarine and sugar together until light and fluffy.
3. Beat in the eggs gradually.
4. Fold in the sieved cinnamon and flour with the apricots and dates.
5. Fold in the orange rind and juice.
6. Turn into prepared soufflé dish. Level the top.
7. Microwave, uncovered, on 60%/MEDIUM for 5 minutes.
8. Sprinkle the nuts evenly over the part-cooked cake. Return to the microwave, giving the dish a ½-turn.

9. Microwave, uncovered, on 60%/MEDIUM for about 3 minutes, or until cake is well risen and just set.

10. Allow to stand for 10–15 minutes, then turn out on to two sheets of kitchen roll, arranged on a cooling rack.

11. When the cake is quite cold, turn right way up again and serve.

* The almonds may be toasted in the microwave. Simply arrange them, spread out, on a tea-plate and microwave, uncovered, on 100%/FULL power for 2–3 minutes or until lightly coloured. Rearrange once or twice during cooking. Set aside until cold before sprinkling on the cake.

APRICOT CHEESE

Dried apricots are a particularly good source of dietary fibre. They also supply the body with iron, calcium and vitamin A, the anti-infective vitamin. The low-fat cheese is light to digest and low in calories.

PREPARATION TIME (after assembling ingredients):
    5 minutes
MICROWAVE COOKING TIME: 10 minutes
SERVES: 4–6

225g (8oz) no-need-to-soak dried apricots, rinsed
150g (6oz) quark (skimmed milk soft cheese)

1 × 15ml spoon (1 tablespoon) castor sugar
50–75g (2–3oz) toasted almond nibs

1. Put the apricots into a 1.7 litre (3 pint) bowl. Cover with boiling water and then cover with a lid.

2. Microwave on 100%/FULL power for 10 minutes. Set aside, covered, until cool.

3. Put the quark into a food processor or liquidizer. Using a draining spoon, lift the apricots and add to the quark. Add the sugar.

4. Add 115ml (4fl oz) cooking liquid from the apricots and process until smooth.

141

5. Turn into individual serving dishes and chill until ready to serve.
6. Serve sprinkled with almond nibs.

* The almond nibs may be toasted in the microwave. Simply arrange them, spread out, on a tea-plate and microwave, uncovered, on 100%/FULL power for 2–3 minutes, or until lightly coloured. Rearrange once or twice during cooking and set aside until cold before sprinkling over the dessert.

CAROB-COATED WHOLEMEAL STRAWBERRY SHORTCAKE

Wholemeal flour adds fibre and a delicious nutty flavour to shortbread, which is made here with polyunsaturated margarine. Carob is healthier than chocolate, and mixed with low-fat soft cheese it produces an excellent topping. Carob chips are available from the health food shop.

PREPARATION TIME (after assembling ingredients):
  10 minutes
MICROWAVE COOKING TIME: 8–9 minutes
SERVES: 4

oil for greasing
100g (4oz) polyunsaturated margarine, straight from fridge
50g (2oz) soft light-brown sugar
175g (6oz) wholemeal plain flour

50g (2oz) carob chips
50g (2oz) quark (low-fat soft cheese)
225g (½lb) fresh strawberries, hulled and halved

1. Lightly oil a 1.7 litre (3 pint) reusable microwave soufflé dish.
2. Work together the margarine and sugar until combined. Gradually work in the flour to form a pliable dough.
3. Press the dough into the prepared container, using your hands.
4. Refrigerate for 10 minutes, then prick all over with a fork.

5. Microwave on 100%/FULL power for about 5 minutes, giving the dish a ½-turn twice during cooking.

6. Allow to stand in the container for 15 minutes, then turn out and cool on a rack.

7. Put the carob chips into a 1.7 litre (3 pint) mixing bowl. Microwave, uncovered, on 40%/SIMMER for 2–3 minutes, or until melted. Stir during cooking.

8. Gradually beat the quark into the melted carob.

9. Spread over the shortbread and, just before the topping has set, decorate with the hulled, halved strawberries. Cut into triangles to serve.

* Carob, like chocolate, tends to melt in its shape and so it is important to stir during and at the end of cooking.

PLUM CRUMBLE

This healthy crumble uses oats, nuts and wholemeal flour to provide a textured topping for the plums. Victoria plums have an excellent flavour, but if they are not available any type of plum may be used.

PREPARATION TIME (after assembling ingredients):
  20 minutes
MICROWAVE COOKING TIME: 10 minutes + grilling time
SERVES: 4

550g (1¼lb) English eating plums, preferably Victoria
1 × 15ml spoon (1 tablespoon) muscovado sugar

FOR THE TOPPING
75g (3oz) polyunsaturated margarine
75g (3oz) medium rolled oats

25g (1oz) wheatgerm
75g (3oz) shelled, husked peanuts
75g (3oz) wholemeal flour, plain
50g (2oz) dark demerara sugar
grated rind of 1 lemon

1. Wash, halve and stone the plums, put them into a deep dish, and sprinkle over the sugar.

2. Put the margarine into a 1.7 litre (3 pint) mixing bowl and microwave on 70%/ROAST for about 2 minutes, or until melted.
3. Stir in all the remaining ingredients.
4. Sprinkle the crumble mixture over the prepared plums.
5. Microwave, uncovered, on 100%/FULL power for about 8 minutes, or until the plums and topping are cooked.
6. Allow to stand for 5 minutes, then brown under a pre-heated grill and serve with ice cream or yoghurt.

RASPBERRY AND APPLE MOUSSE

Raspberries are high in fibre and vitamin C. They have a lovely light flavour. This mousse uses yoghurt and apple purée instead of cream. A low-fat dessert.

PREPARATION TIME (after assembling ingredients):
   15 minutes
MICROWAVE COOKING TIME: 8–11 minutes
SERVES: 4–6

450g (1lb) Bramley cooking apples, peeled and diced
150g (6oz) raspberries, fresh or frozen
3–4 × 15ml (3–4 tablespoons) soft light-brown sugar
1 × 11g (0.4oz) sachet powdered gelatine

2 × 15ml spoons (2 tablespoons) water
140ml (5fl oz) Greek yoghurt
2 large eggs, size 2, separated

TO DECORATE
a few fresh raspberries or apple slices

1. Put the prepared Bramley apples and raspberries into a 1.7 litre (3 pint) casserole with the sugar. Cover and microwave on 100%/FULL power for 6–8 minutes, or until the apples 'fall'. Set aside for 15 minutes, covered.
2. Put the water into a small bowl. Sprinkle the gelatine over the surface and set aside for 15 minutes.
3. Microwave the gelatine for 2–3 minutes on 40%/SIMMER. Stir to ensure the gelatine has dissolved.

4. Pass the fruit through a sieve. Stir the dissolved gelatine into the resulting purée.
5. Allow to cool a little, then stir in the egg yolks, one at a time. Allow to cool completely.
6. Fold in the yoghurt evenly.
7. Whip the egg whites until they hold their shape and fold into the apple mixture.
8. Turn into a serving dish and refrigerate until set.
9. Decorate with a few fresh raspberries or slices of eating apple, with the peel left on, just before serving.

* This is delicious served with the Carob-Coated Wholemeal Strawberry Shortcake on p. 142.

* If you are using frozen raspberries, the fruit may take 1–2 minutes longer to cook in point 1 of the method.

APRICOT AND DATE PUDDING

A super light pudding made with wholemeal breadcrumbs and the minimum of fat. Natural ingredients are used to sweeten the pudding, which should be served hot.

PREPARATION TIME (after assembling ingredients):
   10 minutes
MICROWAVE COOKING TIME: 9–10 minutes
SERVES: 4

100g (4oz) fresh wholemeal breadcrumbs
50g (2oz) medium rolled oats
50g (2oz) polyunsaturated margarine, grated, straight from the fridge
75g (3oz) dried apricots, chopped and soaked

75g (3oz) dates, chopped
1 × 15ml spoon (1 tablespoon) honey, level
1 egg, size 3
140ml (5fl oz) pure orange juice

1. Put all the dry ingredients into a medium-sized mixing bowl. Fork in the grated margarine. Fork in the drained apricots.

145

2. Beat together the honey, egg and orange juice and add to the dry ingredients. Mix well to combine.
3. Turn into an ungreased 825ml (1½ pint) plastic pudding basin. Cover.
4. Microwave on 40%/SIMMER for 7 minutes. Give the dish a ½-turn, then continue to microwave on 100%/FULL power for 2–3 minutes, or until the pudding is cooked.
5. Allow to stand for 5–10 minutes, then turn out on to a serving dish and serve.

* The Lemon Sauce below is excellent with this pudding.

* The chopped, dried apricots should be put into a medium bowl, covered with cold water and allowed to stand for 2 hours at room temperature, then drained, before being used in this recipe.

TANGY LEMON SAUCE

This sauce made from fresh lemons and honey contains vitamin C. It is thickened with arrowroot, which produces a clear result. A delicious sauce that may be served with many desserts.

PREPARATION TIME (after assembling ingredients):
    5 minutes
MICROWAVE COOKING TIME: 3–4 minutes
SERVES: 4

2 × 5ml spoons (2 teaspoons)
    arrowroot, rounded
juice of 2 large lemons

rind of 1 large lemon
1 × 15ml spoon (1 tablespoon)
    runny honey

1. Blend the arrowroot with a little water to a smooth consistency in a large jug.
2. Measure the squeezed lemon juice and make it up to 200ml (7fl oz) with water.
3. Blend the lemon juice and water into the arrowroot mixture.
4. Microwave, uncovered, on 100%/FULL power for 3–4 minutes, stirring frequently, or until the sauce boils and thickens.
5. Stir in the lemon rind and honey. Serve immediately.

APPLE AND PEAR SNOW

Very little sugar is used in this super light recipe which makes a
delicious pudding that everyone will enjoy. A high-fibre, no-fat
recipe that is ideal for weight-watchers.

PREPARATION TIME (after assembling ingredients):
   5 minutes
MICROWAVE COOKING TIME: 6 minutes
SERVES: 4

450g (1lb) Bramley cooking
   apples, peeled, cored and
   sliced
2 ripe Conference eating
   pears, peeled, cored and
   chopped

50g (2oz) soft light-brown
   sugar
2 egg whites
zest of 1 orange – either grate
   the peel or use a zester

1. Put the prepared fruit into a large bowl. Sprinkle over the
    sugar.
2. Cover and microwave on 100%/FULL power for about 6
    minutes, or until the fruit is tender. Stir once after 3
    minutes.
3. Set aside until cool.
4. Turn into a food processor or liquidizer and process until
    smooth.
5. Return to the bowl and set aside until quite cold. Alterna-
    tively, the fruit may be sieved.
6. Whip the egg white until standing in soft peaks.
7. Fold the egg white into the fruit purée and turn into
    individual sundae dishes. Top with orange zest.
8. Chill well before serving.

*   A 'zester' is a very useful tool for removing the 'zest' only of all citrus
    fruits. They are inexpensive and now available from most kitchen
    shops.

SPICED APPLES AND PEARS

A quick and simple sweet, ideal to make in the autumn, when there is plenty of English fruit about. A high-fibre dessert which uses the minimum of sugar.

PREPARATION TIME (after assembling ingredients):
15 minutes
MICROWAVE COOKING TIME: 5–7 minutes
SERVES: 4

2 Bramley cooking apples, each weighing 180g (6oz)
3 Conference eating pears, ripe
2 × 15ml spoons (2 tablespoons) medium-dry white wine *or* 2 × 15ml spoons (2 tablespoons) pure apple juice
1 × 15ml spoon (1 tablespoon) soft brown sugar, rounded

½ × 5ml spoon (½ teaspoon) ground cloves
2–3 × 15ml spoons (2–3 tablespoons) unsweetened desiccated coconut, rounded
50g (2oz) walnuts, chopped } mixed

1. Peel and core the apples and pears, cut into chunks and put into a round pie dish.
2. Mix together the wine or apple juice, sugar and cloves.
3. Pour over the fruit. Cover and microwave on 100%/FULL power for 5–7 minutes, or until the fruit is tender. Stir and re-cover twice during this time.
4. Set aside for 5 minutes, then serve sprinkled with the shredded coconut and walnuts.

* Also delicious cold, but if serving chilled add the topping just before serving.

LEMON AND LIME CURD

On a healthy diet jams, marmalades and fruit curds should not feature excessively. However, a little of this 'tangy' spread will not do anyone any harm. It's so easy to prepare in the microwave and a good source of vitamin C.

PREPARATION TIME (after assembling ingredients):
15 minutes
MICROWAVE COOKING TIME: 12–14 minutes
SERVES: makes about 1.25g (2½lb)

rind and juice of 3 large
  lemons, scrubbed clean
rind and juice of 3 limes,
  scrubbed clean

225g (8oz) polyunsaturated
  margarine
500g (1lb) demerara sugar
5 eggs, size 2, beaten

1. Microwave the scrubbed fruit on a dinner-plate for 2 minutes on 100%/FULL power. This will allow the maximum amount of juice to be extracted.
2. Put the margarine into a 2.3 litre (4 pint) mixing bowl and microwave on 70%/ROAST for 3–4 minutes, or until melted. Stir once or twice during this time.
3. Beat together the eggs and sugar and the rind and juice from the lemons and limes. Add to the melted margarine.
4. Cook for 7–8 minutes on 100%/FULL power, or until thickened.
5. Stir every minute.
6. Pour into sterilized jars. Seal and label.

* The frequent stirring is extremely important if you don't want to end up with scrambled eggs! I use a balloon whisk.

* *To sterilize jars:* Fill the jars two-thirds full with hot water. Microwave all three together, uncovered, on 100%/FULL power until the water is boiling. Let stand for 10 minutes. Then, USING OVEN GLOVES, carefully pour off the water, being careful not to touch the rims of the jars. Fill and seal as normal, and label when cold.

BRANDY BANANAS WITH ORANGE

Bananas are a good source of vitamin C. They are high in fibre and mainly comprise carbohydrate. A cooked banana has a very different flavour to the raw variety and they make delicious hot sweets. Serve immediately after cooking.

PREPARATION TIME (after assembling ingredients):
5 minutes

MICROWAVE COOKING TIME: 4 minutes
SERVES: 4

3 large, firm bananas
25g (1oz) polyunsaturated
  margarine
1 × 15ml spoon (1 tablespoon)
  muscovado sugar
1 × 15ml spoon (1 tablespoon)
  brandy

rind and juice of ½ a large
  orange, scrubbed clean

FOR DECORATION
1 orange, sliced

1. Peel and slice the bananas.
2. Put the margarine into a fairly shallow serving dish and
    microwave for 1 minute on 100%/FULL power, or until
    melted.
3. Add the bananas and sugar. Stir gently.
4. Microwave, uncovered, on 100%/FULL power for 2 minutes,
    stirring after 1 minute and again at the end of the cooking
    time.
5. Add the brandy with the rind and juice of the orange.
6. Microwave, covered, on 100%/FULL power for 1 minute.
    Stir.
7. Serve immediately garnished with the remaining orange,
    sliced and accompanied by Greek yoghurt.

WHOLEFOOD CAROB CAKE

Carob powder is healthier than cocoa as it does not contain
caffeine and theobromine and is higher in natural sugar, fibre
and iron. Serve this cake with the apricot filling, simply
sprinkled with a little desiccated coconut, or top it with the
carob topping suggested for the Shortcake recipe on p. 142.

PREPARATION TIME (after assembling ingredients):
  15 minutes
MICROWAVE COOKING TIME: 12–13 minutes
SERVES: 6–8

150g (6oz) polyunsaturated
   margarine
150g (6oz) dark muscovado
   brown sugar
125g (5oz)
   wholewheat
   self-raising   } mixed
   flour   together
25g (1oz) carob
   powder, sieved)

3 eggs, size 3, beaten with
   2 × 15ml spoons (2
   tablespoons) semi-skimmed
   milk
100g (4oz) dried apricots,
   chopped roughly

FOR THE FILLING
low-sugar apricot jam

FOR DECORATION
a little desiccated coconut

1. Lightly grease a large Anchor Hocking microwave ring mould 23cm (9in) across.
2. Beat together the margarine and sugar until the mixture is light and fluffy. Gradually beat in the egg and milk mixture, adding a small amount of flour with each addition of egg to prevent the mixture curdling.
3. Fold in the remaining flour with the drained apricots.
4. Microwave, uncovered, on 70%/ROAST for 12–13 minutes, or until the cake is well risen and just set. Give the container a ¼-turn two or three times during cooking.
5. Allow to stand in container for 20 minutes, then turn out on to a double sheet of absorbent kitchen paper which has been sprinkled with a little desiccated coconut. Allow to cool.
6. When quite cold, turn the cake over, split in two horizontally, and fill with apricot jam. Sandwich together again and serve sprinkled with a little extra desiccated coconut.

* If possible, the dried apricots should be covered with cold water and set aside for 2 hours, then drained, before being used in this recipe.

BLACKCURRANT AND APPLE WHIP

The flavour of blackcurrants predominates in this high-fibre, low-fat dessert, full of vitamin C. I serve this with the Fruity Walnut Flapjacks recipe on p. 171.

PREPARATION TIME (after assembling ingredients):
5 minutes

MICROWAVE COOKING TIME: 8–10 minutes
SERVES: 6

450g (1lb) Bramley cooking
   apples, peeled and sliced
225g (8oz) frozen
   blackcurrants
2 × 15ml spoons (2
   tablespoons) soft brown
   sugar, level

3 × 15ml spoons (3
   tablespoons) runny honey
150g (5.29oz) natural yoghurt,
   thick-set
2 egg whites, size 2

1. Layer the apples and blackcurrants into a large casserole
   dish with the sugar.
2. Cover and microwave on 100%/FULL power for 8–10 minutes, or until the fruit is soft. Stir and re-cover after 5
   minutes.
3. Set aside, covered, for 10–15 minutes then pass through a
   sieve. Stir in the honey and leave to cool.
4. Blend in the yoghurt until smooth.
5. Beat the egg whites until stiff and fold in.
6. Turn into individual sundae dishes and refrigerate until
   ready to serve. (Eat within 2 hours of preparation.)

YOGHURT CREAM

The oranges are microwaved briefly first so that they will yield
the maximum amount of juice. Honey is used as a sweetener for
its delicious flavour. This delicious dessert is low in fat and high
in vitamin C, and makes an easily digested dessert, especially
useful after a dinner party.

PREPARATION TIME (after assembling ingredients):
   15 minutes
MICROWAVE COOKING TIME: 4½–5 minutes
SERVES: 4

2 medium oranges
1 × 15ml spoon (1 tablespoon)
   runny honey

225g (8oz) natural yoghurt,
   thick-set
a small red-skinned apple
   (Discovery, if possible)

1 × 11g (0.4oz) sachet
  powdered gelatine
1 nectarine *or* 1 banana

FOR THE SAUCE
225g (8oz) raspberries,
  defrosted if frozen

1 × 15ml spoon (1 tablespoon)
  runny honey

TO DECORATE
100g (4oz) fresh strawberries,
  halved

1. Put the oranges on to a plate and microwave on 100%/ FULL power for 1 minute.
2. Grate the peel from 1 orange into a bowl. Add the juice from both oranges. Measure this juice and make it up to 170ml (6fl oz) with water if necessary.
3. Microwave the orange juice and rind for 2 minutes on 20%/WARM. Stir in the honey to dissolve, then set aside until cold.
4. Sprinkle the gelatine on to 2 × 15ml spoons (2 tablespoons) cold water. Allow to stand for 5 minutes, then microwave on 40%/SIMMER for 1½–2 minutes. Stir to ensure the gelatine has dissolved.
5. Stir the dissolved gelatine into the orange juice mixture.
6. Turn the yoghurt into a bowl. Gradually stir in the orange juice, blending well.
7. Wash the apple and the nectarine, and chop roughly, discarding the nectarine stone and the core of the apple, but do not peel the fruit. If using a banana, peel and slice.
8. Fold the prepared fruit into the yoghurt mixture.
9. With cold water rinse a reusable 1.7 litre (3 pint) microwave soufflé dish, which you can use as a mould.
10. Fill the dish with the yoghurt cream and refrigerate to set.
11. Prepare the sauce: Simply pass the raspberries through a sieve and stir the honey into the resulting purée.
12. To serve: Hold the set 'cream' in a bowl of very hot water and count to seven. Hold the serving plate over the mould, turn it over, and shake until the yoghurt cream releases itself.
13. Serve immediately topped with the raspberry sauce and decorated with the fresh strawberry halves.

INDIVIDUAL WALNUT SPONGES

These low-fat sponges have an excellent flavour. The texture of the sponge is extremely light. Serve them on their own or make a sauce from a reduced-sugar apricot jam. Simply stir a little water into the jam in a jug and microwave, uncovered, until hot. Stir before serving.

PREPARATION TIME (after assembling ingredients): 15–20 minutes
MICROWAVE COOKING TIME: 5½–6½ minutes
SERVES: 4

25g (1oz) butter
3 eggs, size 2
75g (3oz) soft light-brown sugar
50g (2oz) ground almonds
25g (1oz) semolina

25g (1oz) walnuts, chopped fairly finely
25g (1oz) wholewheat flour, plain
½ × 5ml spoon (½ teaspoon) pure almond essence

1. Microwave the butter in a small bowl on 40%/SIMMER for about 1½ minutes, or until melted. Set aside.
2. Very lightly grease 4 × 285ml (4 × ½ pint) individual plastic pudding basins with a little of the butter. Retain the remainder.
3. Beat together the eggs and sugar, using an electric whisk if possible, until really thick and creamy – it takes about 6 minutes with my Chefette mixer. When you lift the whisk, the mixture should fall and leave a trail in the basin.
4. Using a tablespoon, fold the ground almonds, semolina, almond essence, chopped walnuts and wholewheat flour into the mixture.
5. Lastly, fold in the melted butter.
6. Divide the mixture evenly between the prepared pudding basins.
7. Microwave, uncovered, on 70%/ROAST for 4–5 minutes, giving the puddings a ¼-turn twice during the cooking time.
8. Allow to stand for 3–4 minutes, then turn out and serve hot.

154

Apricot Brûlé

Apricots are high in fibre. When cooked in orange juice they have a clean tangy flavour. This lower-fat version of a brûlé will prove very popular with young and old alike. The dried apricots should be covered with cold water and set aside for 2 hours before being used in this recipe.

PREPARATION TIME (after assembling ingredients):
   10 minutes
MICROWAVE COOKING TIME:
   8–10 minutes + grilling time
SERVES: 4

100g (4oz) dried apricots
about 170ml (6fl oz) pure
   orange juice
2.5cm (1in) piece cinnamon
   stick

150g (5.29oz) natural yoghurt,
   thick-set
70ml (2½fl oz) soured cream
75g (3oz) demerara sugar

1. Drain the apricots after soaking and put into a 1.7 litre (3 pint) bowl. Add the cinnamon stick.
2. Pour over the orange juice so that it just covers the fruit.
3. Cover and microwave on 100%/FULL power for 8–10 minutes, or until the fruit is tender.
4. Set aside until cool.
5. Using a draining spoon, lift the apricots and divide evenly between 4 ramekin dishes. Add 1 × 15ml spoon (1 tablespoon) of the orange juice to each ramekin. (Reserve the remaining orange juice and use to make into a sauce for another dessert.)
6. Blend together the yoghurt and soured cream and spoon evenly over the apricots.
7. Divide the sugar between the ramekins, sprinkling it over the yoghurt and soured cream mixture to cover.
8. Flash under a pre-heated grill until the sugar caramelizes – watch continuously.
9. Chill in the fridge for an hour before serving.

BROWN RICE PUDDING

High-fibre brown rice makes a delicious nutty pudding. Served with dates and a little nutmeg, this low-fat dessert is delicious hot or cold.

PREPARATION TIME (after assembling ingredients):
  5 minutes
MICROWAVE COOKING TIME: 46–51 minutes
SERVES: 4

550ml (1 pint) semi-skimmed milk

100g (4oz) natural brown American rice

25g (1oz) light muscovado sugar

75g (3oz) stoned dates, chopped

3–4 × 15ml spoons (3–4 tablespoons) evaporated milk

TO SERVE
a little grated nutmeg

1. Put the milk into a 2.3 litre (4 pint) bowl or casserole. Cover and microwave for 6 minutes on 100%/FULL power.
2. Stir in the brown rice with the sugar. Cover and microwave on 70%/ROAST for 40–45 minutes.
3. Stir and set aside for 10 minutes.
4. Stir in the dates with the evaporated milk.
5. Serve hot sprinkled with the grated nutmeg.

* If serving cold, stir in a little extra semi-skimmed milk or evaporated milk, then sprinkle with nutmeg. Cover and allow to cool.

SEMOLINA WITH CHERRIES

A light milk pudding served with cherries, which are naturally sweet and need no added sugar. An ideal dessert on a cold winter's day that all the family will enjoy. This pud is high in fibre and also provides protein.

PREPARATION TIME (after assembling ingredients):
5 minutes
MICROWAVE COOKING TIME: 13–16 minutes
SERVES: 4–6

225g (8oz) pitted dark sweet cherries, frozen
600ml (1 pint) semi-skimmed milk
4 × 15ml spoons (4 tablespoons) semolina, level

50g (2oz) soft light-brown sugar
1 egg, size 2, beaten

TO SERVE
a little grated nutmeg

1. Put the cherries into a 1.1 litre (2 pint) serving dish and microwave on 30%/DEFROST for 5–6 minutes. Stir and set aside.
2. Stir the milk and semolina into a 1.7 litre (3 pint) mixing bowl.
3. Cover and microwave on 100%/FULL power for 8–10 minutes, or until boiling and thickened. Stir frequently during cooking.
4. Stir in the sugar and allow to stand for 10 minutes. Stir in the beaten egg and pour over the defrosted cherries.
5. Serve sprinkled with the grated nutmeg.

* This dessert is also delicious served cold.

CHILDREN'S MENUS

It is important to educate children's palates towards healthy eating. They will then naturally pursue a healthy diet as they mature. These twelve, two-course menus have been designed to appeal to children who will not realize how nutritionally sound they are. The minute you start telling children that they should eat a meal as it is healthy and good for them, you start having problems!

Encourage older children to help with the preparation and cooking of food, especially with the microwave, which is so easy for them to use.

Serve small portions in attractive dishes that show you care about what they eat, and don't put the salt cellar on the table!

VEGETABLE SOUP WITH SHISH KEBAB

Lean chuck steak or fillet of lamb is combined with wholemeal breadcrumbs and seasonings to make these tasty meatballs. Add them to the high-fibre soup and you have plenty of protein to make this a complete meal for four hungry children.

PREPARATION TIME (after assembling ingredients):
   20–30 minutes
MICROWAVE COOKING TIME: 39 minutes
SERVES: 4

FOR THE SHISH KEBAB
150g (6oz) raw minced chuck steak or leg of lamb fillet, minced
1 spring onion, or 1 pickling onion, finely chopped
25g (1oz) wholemeal breadcrumbs
1 × 5ml spoon (1 teaspoon) lemon juice

1 × 5ml spoon (1 teaspoon) mild curry powder, level
1 × 5ml spoon (1 teaspoon) dried parsley, level
1 × 15ml spoon (1 tablespoon) natural yoghurt
2 × 5ml spoons (2 teaspoons) soya sauce

FOR THE SOUP
1 onion, finely chopped
1 stick celery, chopped
1 × 150g (6oz) potato, peeled
   and diced
2 medium courgettes, sliced
1 carrot, diced
4 large ripe tomatoes, peeled,
   deseeded and chopped *or a*
   220g can chopped tomatoes

1 × 5ml spoon (1 teaspoon)
   dried oregano
2 × 15ml spoons (2
   tablespoons) tomato
   purée, level
700ml (1¼ pints) beef stock,
   cold
140ml (¼ pint) milk
freshly ground black pepper

1. Make the shish kebabs: Combine all the ingredients in a large mixing bowl.
2. Form into 16 balls, each about the size of a walnut. Arrange them on a microwave roasting rack, leaving a space right in the centre.
3. Microwave, uncovered, on 70%/ROAST for about 6 minutes. Set aside. Cover and keep warm.
4. Make the soup: Put the onion, celery, potato, courgettes and carrot into a 2.3 litre (4 pint) container.
5. Cover and microwave on 100%/FULL power for 8 minutes, stirring and re-covering after 4 minutes.
6. Stir in all remaining ingredients.
7. Cover and microwave on 100%/FULL power for 20 minutes.
8. Allow to stand for 5 minutes. Then, using a draining spoon, carefully transfer the vegetables to a food processor or liquidizer.
9. Add 1 cupful of the liquid. Process until smooth.
10. Return to the container, blending the processed vegetables into the remaining liquid.
11. Microwave on 100%/FULL power for 5 minutes. Stir.
12. Divide the soup between four warmed soup bowls. Add 4 shish kebabs to each bowl and serve immediately.

* Older children may like the soup served sprinkled with plenty of freshly chopped parsley.

MUESLI CRUMBLE

This high-fibre dessert cooks very quickly in the microwave. Blackcurrants and bananas combine well, and blackcurrants provide vitamin C. Serve the crumble hot or cold with plain yoghurt.

> PREPARATION TIME (after assembling ingredients):
>   10 minutes
> MICROWAVE COOKING TIME: 7 minutes
> SERVES: 4

450g (1lb) blackcurrants, topped and tailed, or frozen
2 medium bananas, sliced
50g (2oz) light muscovado sugar
150g (6oz) unsweetened dry muesli

FOR THE TOPPING
50g (2oz) polyunsaturated margarine
25g (1oz) demerara sugar
grated rind of 1 lemon

1. Prepare the topping: Put the margarine into a 1.7 litre (3 pint) mixing bowl and microwave on 100%/FULL power for about 1 minute or until melted. Stir in the muesli and set aside.
2. Arrange the blackcurrants with the sliced banana in a 1.1 litre (2 pint) casserole. Sprinkle over the muscovado sugar.
3. Add the demerara sugar and lemon rind to the topping. Mix well.
4. Sprinkle the prepared topping evenly over the fruit.
5. Do not cover. Microwave on 100%/FULL power for about 6 minutes or until the blackcurrants are soft.
6. Serve immediately, or it may be served cold.

PITTA BREAD WITH BAKED BEANS AND EDAM

High-fibre wholewheat pitta bread, filled with baked beans and cheese, both of which provide protein. An extremely quick to cook snack that is filling and nutritious, and low in fat too.

PREPARATION TIME (after assembling ingredients):
  5 minutes
MICROWAVE COOKING TIME: 5–6 minutes
SERVES: 4

4 large wholewheat pitta
  breads

FOR THE FILLING
1 small onion, chopped
1 × 440g (15.5oz) can Crosse &
  Blackwell Healthy Balance
  baked beans in
  reduced-salt-and-sugar
  tomato sauce

½ × 5ml spoon (½ teaspoon)
  ground cumin
150g (6oz) Edam cheese, cubed

1. Put the onion into a 1.7 litre (3 pint) mixing bowl and microwave on 100%/FULL power for 1 minute.
2. Stir in the baked beans with the cumin. Cover and microwave for 4–5 minutes on 70%/ROAST. Stir after 2 minutes and at the end of heating.
3. Stir in the cubed Edam.
4. Slice open the pittas and fill evenly with the baked bean mixture.
5. Serve immediately with a salad made from apple, celery and cucumber.

LEMON MOUSSE

This light, tangy mousse provides vitamin C. A low-calorie dessert that may be made in advance. Perfect after almost any meal.

PREPARATION TIME (after assembling ingredients):
25 minutes

MICROWAVE COOKING TIME: 3–4 minutes

SERVES: 4–6

the rind and juice of 2 large
  lemons
1 × 11g (0.4oz) sachet
  powdered gelatine
3 eggs, size 2, separated

2 × 15ml spoons (2
  tablespoons) castor
  sugar, level
55ml (2fl oz) evaporated milk

1. Arrange the lemons on a plate and microwave on 100%/
   FULL power for 1 minute.
2. Sprinkle the gelatine over 2 × 15ml spoons (2 tablespoons)
   cold water and leave to soak for 5 minutes.
3. Mix together the egg yolks, sugar and lemon rind. Beat
   with an electric mixer until thick, pale and creamy.
4. Juice the lemons and add the strained juice to the soaked
   gelatine.
5. Microwave the lemon juice and soaked gelatine on 40%/
   SIMMER for 2–3 minutes. Stir to ensure the gelatine has
   dissolved.
6. Pour the dissolved gelatine into the whipped egg yolk
   mixture, beating continually. Set aside for 15 minutes.
7. Whip the evaporated milk until thick, then beat it into the
   egg yolk mixture. Continue to whisk for about 2 minutes.
8. Lastly, whip the egg whites in a clean bowl until stiff.
9. Using a metal spoon, fold the whipped egg whites into the
   lemon mixture.
10. Spoon into individual serving dishes and refrigerate until
    ready to serve.

HEALTHY BURGERS

By extending the minced steak with bulgar wheat, and cooking
the burgers on a microwave roasting rack to drain away fat
expelled during cooking, these burgers become a very healthy

main meal for any child. Bulgar wheat is available from the health food shop.

PREPARATION TIME (after assembling ingredients):
10–15 minutes
MICROWAVE COOKING TIME: 8–10 minutes
SERVES: 5

5 white or wholemeal burger
  rolls with sesame seeds

FOR THE FILLING
40g (1½oz) bulgar wheat
200g (8oz) minced chuck steak
2 × 15ml spoons (2
  tablespoons) cooked lentils

1 small onion, finely chopped
1 × 5ml spoon (1 teaspoon)
  Bovril, level
1 × 5ml spoon (1 teaspoon)
  dried parsley
1 small egg
freshly ground black pepper

1. Put the bulgar wheat into a medium bowl. Cover with cold water and leave to soak for 15–20 minutes.
2. Drain through a sieve, pressing out excess water with a wooden spoon.
3. Turn the drained bulgar wheat into a clean medium-sized bowl.
4. Add all the remaining ingredients and mix well.
5. Divide the mixture into 5 and shape into burgers.
6. Arrange on a microwave roasting rack.
7. Microwave on 70%/ROAST for 8–10 minutes, turning each burger over once, half-way through.
8. Split the baps and fill each one with a burger.
9. Serve immediately with a mixed salad.

BLACKBERRY AND APPLE PANCAKES

Pancakes made with semi-skimmed milk and wholemeal flour are a good start to healthy eating. Fill them with colourful blackberry and apple, cooked with a little honey instead of sugar, and children will love this high-fibre dessert that is also good for them.

PREPARATION TIME (after assembling ingredients):
12 minutes

MICROWAVE COOKING TIME: 15–19 minutes

SERVES: 6

6 wholemeal pancakes, frozen
(see recipe for Crab
Pancakes on p. 22)
675g (1½lb) Bramley cooking
apples, peeled, cored and
sliced

225g (8oz) blackberries, fresh
or frozen
2 × 15ml spoon (2 tablespoons)
runny honey, level

1. Microwave the frozen pancakes for 5–7 minutes on DE-FROST. Stand for 5 minutes. They will now be almost thawed and easy to handle.
2. Meanwhile cook the filling. Layer the blackberries and apples in a 1.7 litre (3 pint) casserole. Add the honey.
3. Cover and microwave on 100%/FULL power for 8–10 minutes, or until cooked. Stir and re-cover twice during cooking.
4. Allow to stand for 10 minutes, then carefully divide the filling between the pancakes. Roll them up and arrange in a suitable dish.
5. Cover and microwave on 100%/FULL power for about 2 minutes to reheat.
6. Serve immediately with low-fat ice cream or yoghurt.

* If you find the resulting stewed fruit is a little wet, carefully pour off the surplus liquid and serve in a jug.

RICE WITH HAM

There is little washing up after this high-fibre, low-fat dish as it is cooked in one pot. Raisins and apricots provide fibre, and also make the dish visually appealing to children. Lightly spiced and cooked in stock, this is an excellent way of introducing children to brown rice.

PREPARATION TIME (after assembling ingredients):
  10–15 minutes
MICROWAVE COOKING TIME: 34 minutes
SERVES: 4

2 large onions, chopped
½ a green pepper, cut into
  strips
1 carrot, cut into matchsticks
1 clove garlic, chopped
  (optional)
150g (6oz) brown rice
550ml (1 pint) well-flavoured
  chicken stock, hot
½ × 5ml spoon (½ teaspoon)
  dried oregano

freshly ground black pepper
1 × 5ml spoon (1 teaspoon)
  ground ginger
25g (1oz) raisins
25g (1oz) dried apricots
100g (4oz) lean, diced ham or 4
  hard-boiled eggs, chopped

TO SERVE
plenty of freshly chopped
  parsley

1. Put the onions, green pepper, carrot and garlic into a 2.3
    litre (4 pint) casserole. Cover and microwave on 100%/FULL
    power for 4 minutes, stirring after 2 minutes.
2. Stir in the rice, stock and oregano with the black pepper and
    ground ginger.
3. Cover and microwave on 100%/FULL power for 30 minutes,
    without removing the lid.
4. Let stand for 15 minutes, then fork up and add the raisins
    and apricots, and the ham or chopped hard-boiled egg.
5. Turn into a serving dish and serve immediately, sprinkled
    with the chopped parsley.

BLACKBERRY AND BLACKCURRANT FOOL

An excellent light dessert to follow the Rice with Ham. High in
fibre and vitamin C, this dessert has a wonderful flavour and a
rich taste. Serve with wholemeal biscuits or sponge fingers.

PREPARATION TIME (after assembling ingredients):
  15–20 minutes
MICROWAVE COOKING TIME: 8–12 minutes
SERVES: 4–6

225g (8oz) blackcurrants,
  stalks removed, fresh or
  frozen
225g (8oz) blackberries, fresh
  or frozen
50g (2oz) light muscovado
  sugar
1 rounded dessertspoon
  custard powder

1 level dessertspoon demerara
  sugar
225ml (8fl oz) semi-skimmed
  milk
150ml (5fl oz) natural yoghurt,
  thick-set

1. Put the blackcurrants and blackberries into a 2.3 litre (4 pint) bowl or casserole. Add the muscovado sugar.
2. Cover and microwave on 100%/FULL power for 5–8 minutes or until the fruit is soft. Stir.
3. Set aside for 20 minutes, covered.
4. Make the custard: In a 550ml (1 pint) jug blend the custard powder with a little milk. Add the remaining milk.
5. Microwave, uncovered, on 100%/FULL power for 3–4 minutes, or until boiling and thickened. Stir frequently during cooking. Stir in the demerara sugar. Set aside.
6. Put the yoghurt into a large bowl. Pass the fruit through a sieve and blend into the yoghurt.
7. Finally, stir in the prepared custard. Turn into a serving dish and allow to cool.
8. Refrigerate until ready to serve.

CHILLI CON CARNE

The ground semolina will not be noticed, but it 'stretches' the meat to make it go further and so produces a healthy version of this very popular dish. Kidney beans are high in fibre and chuck steak is minced as it is far lower in fat than ordinary mince. Either ask your butcher to mince it for you or do it yourself with a food processor.

PREPARATION TIME (after assembling ingredients):
  10 minutes
MICROWAVE COOKING TIME: 15 minutes
SERVES: 4

1 onion, chopped
1 rasher lean back bacon,
    chopped
225g (8oz) chuck steak, all
    visible fat removed, minced
1 × 15ml spoon (1 tablespoon)
    semolina
100g (4oz) mushrooms, finely
    chopped
½–1 × 5ml spoon (½–1
    teaspoon) chilli powder
1 × 5ml spoon (1 teaspoon)
    dried oregano
2 × 15ml spoon (2 tablespoons)
    tomato purée
1 × 227g (8oz) can chopped
    tomatoes
freshly ground black pepper
400g can red kidney beans,
    drained
2 × 15ml spoons (2
    tablespoons) stock or water

1. Pre-heat a deep microwave browning dish, without the lid, for 3 minutes if it is the small size or for 5 minutes if it is the large.
2. Put the onion and bacon into the dish. Cover and microwave on 100%/FULL power for 1 minute.
3. Add the minced beef and stir. Microwave, covered, on 100%/FULL power for 2 minutes.
4. Add all the remaining ingredients, stirring well.
5. Cover and microwave on 70%/ROAST for 12 minutes, stirring and re-covering after 5 minutes.
6. Stir and serve with wholemeal French bread and a green salad.

APPLE AND RASPBERRY CRUMBLE

This high-fibre crumble should be finished off under a pre-heated grill, so remember to use a grill-proof dish in the micro-wave. Children will love the nutty flavour of the wholemeal flour. Apple concentrate is used in the filling instead of sugar.

PREPARATION TIME (after assembling ingredients):
    12 minutes
MICROWAVE COOKING TIME: 8 minutes + grilling
    time
SERVES: 4

FOR THE CRUMBLE TOPPING
100g (4oz) wholewheat flour
50g (2oz) wholewheat
   breadcrumbs, fresh
75g (3 oz) polyunsaturated
   margarine, from the
   refrigerator
2 × 15ml spoons (2
   tablespoons) muscovado
   sugar
1 × 5ml spoon (1 teaspoon)
   mixed spice

FOR THE FRUIT FILLING
2 large Bramley cooking
   apples
100g (4oz) raspberries, fresh
   or frozen
3 × 15ml spoons (3
   tablespoons) apple juice
   concentrate

1. Prepare the topping: Combine the flour and breadcrumbs. Rub in the margarine until the mixture resembles fine breadcrumbs.
2. Fork in the sugar and mixed spice.
3. Prepare the filling: Peel, core and slice the apples thinly into a suitable dish. Add the apple concentrate and raspberries.
4. Sprinkle the crumble topping evenly over the fruit, pressing down gently.
5. Microwave, uncovered, on 100%/FULL power for 8 minutes.
6. Allow to stand for 5 minutes, then pop under a pre-heated grill to crisp and brown the top.

* Apple juice concentrate is available from health food shops. It does not contain sugar and is ideal in this recipe as a substitute for sugar. Children will probably prefer this low-sugar crumble.

WHOLEMEAL BAP PIZZAS

Serve as a healthy snack instead of a main meal. This combination of cheese and tomato on a plain wholemeal roll is quick and easy to prepare and cook – ideal to serve as the children come in hungry after school, and far better than cakes and biscuits.

PREPARATION TIME (after assembling ingredients):
   10 minutes
MICROWAVE COOKING TIME: 8–10 minutes
SERVES: 3 as a main meal, or 6 as a snack

3 wholemeal baps

FOR THE FILLING
1 medium onion, finely
   chopped
2 tomatoes, peeled and
   chopped

1 × 5ml spoon (1 teaspoon)
   Dijon mustard
100g (4oz) Cheddar cheese,
   grated
2 × 15ml spoons (2
   tablespoons) tomato purée

1. Cut the baps in half and arrange in a ring on a suitable baking sheet.
2. Put the onion into a medium bowl. Cover and microwave on 100%/FULL power for 1–2 minutes.
3. Stir in the chopped tomatoes, tomato purée, mustard and Cheddar cheese.
4. Divide the filling evenly between the baps.
5. Microwave, uncovered, on 40%/SIMMER for 7–8 minutes, or until the cheese melts. Serve immediately.

APPLE AND BANANA WITH CAROB SAUCE

Naturally sweet, fresh fruit is the best dessert for any child. Should they need encouragement, serve a choice of fresh fruit with this naturally sweetened carob sauce. The dessert may be served warm or cold.

PREPARATION TIME (after assembling ingredients):
   10 minutes
MICROWAVE COOKING TIME: 4–5 minutes
SERVES: 4

1 × 15ml spoon (1 tablespoon)
   cornflour, rounded
225ml (8fl oz) semi-skimmed
   milk
75g (3oz) carob chips from
   health food shops

2 medium-sized ripe bananas,
   sliced
3 medium-sized red-skinned
   eating apples, cored and
   sliced

1. In a small bowl mix the cornflour to a smooth paste with a little milk.
2. Put the remaining milk with the carob chips into a 1.1 litre (2 pint) jug.

3. Microwave on 100%/FULL power for 2–3 minutes, stirring frequently. Stir to ensure the carob has melted.
4. Stir in the blended cornflour. Microwave on 100%/FULL power for about 2 minutes, stirring every minute.
5. Arrange the fruit in sundae dishes and top with the sauce. Serve warm or cold.

CHICKEN COBBLER

This filling supper dish is very popular with my family. It is a high-fibre, low-fat meal in one pot that appeals to me as it means less washing up afterwards. Just serve a salad – no potatoes needed.

PREPARATION TIME (after assembling ingredients):
    15 minutes
MICROWAVE COOKING TIME: 18–21 minutes
SERVES: 4

1 stick celery, chopped
1 large onion, chopped
1 × 15ml spoon (1 tablespoon)
    wholewheat flour, rounded
425ml (¾ pint) light chicken
    stock, hot
50g (2oz) frozen sweetcorn
50g (2oz) frozen garden peas
450g (1lb) cooked chicken
    meat, chopped

1 × 5ml spoon (1 teaspoon)
    baking powder
40g (1½oz) polyunsaturated
    margarine, straight from the
    refrigerator
½ × 5ml spoon (½ teaspoon)
    dried parsley
50g (2oz) mature Cheddar
    cheese, finely grated
semi-skimmed milk for mixing

FOR THE COBBLER TOPPING
175g (6oz) self-raising
    wholewheat flour

1. Put the celery and onion into a large casserole. Cover and microwave on 100%/FULL power for 4 minutes; stir and re-cover after 2 minutes.
2. Sprinkle on the flour and then gradually stir in the stock, blending well. Microwave on 100%/FULL power for 6–8 minutes, stirring frequently, or until the sauce is boiling rapidly.

3. Stir in sweetcorn, peas and diced chicken. Cover and micro-
    wave on 100%/FULL power for 3 minutes. Stir.
4. Make the scones: Put the flour and baking powder into a 1.7
    litre (3 pint) mixing-bowl. Rub in the margarine and fork in
    the parsley and the grated cheese.
5. Add sufficient milk to mix to a soft dough.
6. Roll the dough out and cut into 6 scones.
7. Arrange them on top of the dish.
8. Cook, uncovered, on 100%/FULL power for 5–6 minutes.
    Serve immediately.

*   My family like this 'crisped' under the grill before serving, so I
    retain a very small amount of the grated cheese when I make the
    scones and sprinkle this over when the dish comes out of the
    microwave. It then goes under the pre-heated grill for a very short
    time to crisp and brown the top of the scones.

FRUITY WALNUT FLAPJACKS

Oats, muscovado sugar, honey, oats and walnuts are all natural
ingredients. The walnuts add fibre and a wonderful flavour to
these crisp biscuits. The flapjacks crisp up on cooling so be
careful not to overcook them. Useful to serve on their own or
with many desserts.

PREPARATION TIME (after assembling ingredients):
    10 minutes
MICROWAVE COOKING TIME: 5–6 minutes
SERVES: makes 8 flapjacks

75g (3oz) polyunsaturated
    margarine
4 × 15ml spoons (4
    tablespoons) runny honey,
    level

25g (1oz) light muscovado
    sugar
150g (6oz) rolled oats
25g (1oz) chopped walnuts or
    almonds
2 ripe bananas, sliced

1. Lightly grease a 23cm (9in) china quiche dish.
2. Put the margarine, honey and sugar into a 1.7 litre (3 pint)
    bowl. Microwave on 100%/FULL power for 1–2 minutes. Stir

to ensure the sugar has dissolved and the margarine has melted.

3. Add the oats and walnuts, stirring to ensure the ingredients are well combined.
4. Turn the mixture into the prepared dish and level the surface.
5. Microwave, uncovered, on 100%/FULL power for 4 minutes, giving the dish a ½-turn once, half-way through cooking.
6. Allow to cool for 10–12 minutes, then carefully cut into triangles. Allow to become quite cold then lift out on to a serving dish.
7. Serve cold, topped with a few slices of banana.

TUNA POTATO LAYER

Fish and potatoes, cooked in a low-fat cheesy sauce and presented with a crisp topping – no child will realize that this is a healthy-eating recipe, but it presents a good balance of protein and carbohydrate with little fat. An economical and filling meal.

PREPARATION TIME (after assembling ingredients):
  15 minutes
MICROWAVE COOKING TIME: 25–31 minutes
SERVES: 4

750g (1½lb) old white potatoes, peeled and sliced thinly
1 × 200g can tuna fish in oil, drained

FOR THE SAUCE
285ml (½ pint) semi-skimmed milk + 2 extra 15ml spoons (2 tablespoons)
2 × 15ml spoons (2 tablespoons) cornflour, level

75g (3oz) reduced-fat Cheddar cheese, grated

FOR THE TOPPING
50g (2oz) crisp breadcrumbs (see note)
25g (1oz) reduced-fat Cheddar cheese, grated

1. Soak the potatoes in cold water to remove surface starch.
2. Meanwhile make the sauce: Use a little of the milk to cream

the cornflour to a smooth paste in a 1.7 litre (3 pint) mixing bowl.

3. Put the remaining milk into a jug and microwave on 100%/FULL power for 2 minutes.

4. Pour the heated milk on to the creamed cornflour, stirring continuously, then microwave on 100%/FULL power, uncovered, for 3–4 minutes, or until boiling and thickened. Stir every minute. Stir in extra milk and cheese.

5. Drain the potato slices well and layer in a large casserole dish with the drained tuna, finishing with a layer of potatoes. (Keep the tuna away from the outside edge of the dish.)

6. Pour the sauce over to coat.

7. Cover and microwave on 70%/ROAST for 20–25 minutes.

8. Set aside to stand for 10 minutes, then serve sprinkled with the mixed cheese and crisp breadcrumbs.

*   Crisp breadcrumbs, white, brown or wholemeal, make an attractive crunchy topping for many savoury dishes. Make the breadcrumbs in your food processor or liquidizer using day-old bread. Then spread them on a baking sheet and dry out in your *conventional* oven when you are going to use it anyway. Remove when crisp and brown, and cool and pack in rigid polythene containers. Keep them in the fridge for up to two weeks.

CAROB MOUSSE

Carob is a natural ingredient that tastes sweet. It is an excellent substitute for chocolate in this recipe, as a delicious mousse may be made without the addition of any sort of sweetener. Carob has no caffeine and is rich in vitamins and minerals.

PREPARATION TIME (after assembling ingredients):
   5 minutes
MICROWAVE COOKING TIME: 5–7 minutes
SERVES: 4–6

125g (5oz) carob chips, stored in refrigerator
4 eggs, size 2, separated

2 × 15ml spoons (2 tablespoons) semi-skimmed milk
1 banana

1. Put the carob chips into a 1.7 litre (3 pint) mixing bowl.
2. Microwave, uncovered, on 40%/SIMMER for about 5–7 minutes, or until the carob has melted. Stir twice during this time.
3. Set aside for 5 minutes, stirring occasionally, then beat the yolks, one at a time, into the melted carob. Continue to beat with a wooden spoon until the mixture is smooth and creamy. Beat in the milk, gradually.
4. Whisk the egg whites until stiff and fold into the carob mixture, using a metal spoon.
5. Turn the mixture into four sundae dishes and refrigerate until set.
6. Decorate each mousse with sliced banana before serving.

CRISPY MACARONI CHEESE

Spinach is a good source of vitamins A and C. This combination of spinach and cheese will appeal to children who sometimes find the flavour of spinach on its own somewhat overpowering. Wholewheat macaroni provides carbohydrate for energy and is high in fibre. It also contains protein.

PREPARATION TIME (after assembling ingredients): 20 minutes
MICROWAVE COOKING TIME: about 17–19 minutes
SERVES: 4–6

175g (6oz) wholewheat macaroni
1 × 5ml spoon (1 teaspoon) olive oil

FOR THE SAUCE
25g (1oz) polyunsaturated margarine
25g (1oz) wholewheat flour
285ml (10fl oz) semi-skimmed milk
100g (4oz) low-fat hard cheese, grated + 1 tablespoon Parmesan

1 × 227g (8oz) block frozen chopped spinach, defrosted
freshly ground black pepper

FOR THE TOPPING
50g (2 oz) crispy breadcrumbs (see note)
1 × 15ml spoon (1 tablespoon) sesame seeds
35g (1½oz) low-fat hard cheese, grated

1. Put the macaroni and olive oil into a 2.3 litre (4 pint) bowl or casserole and pour over a kettleful of boiling water (about 1.4 litres (2½ pints)).
2. Cover and microwave on 100%/FULL power for 10 minutes, stirring and re-covering after 5 minutes. Set aside for 5 minutes, then drain, rinse with boiling water, cover and keep warm.
3. Make the sauce: Put the margarine into a 1 litre jug and microwave on 100%/FULL power for about 45 seconds, or until melted.
4. Stir in the flour. Gradually stir in the milk.
5. Microwave, uncovered, on 100%/FULL power for about 4 minutes, beating with a balloon whisk after 2 minutes and at the end of the cooking time. Stir in the cheese to melt.
6. Season with the black pepper and fold in the drained spinach – the defrosted spinach must be put into a sieve and the excess water pushed out with the back of a spoon before using.
7. Pour the prepared sauce over the macaroni.
8. Combine the remaining cheese, breadcrumbs and sesame seeds and sprinkle evenly over the top.
9. Microwave, uncovered, on 100%/FULL power for about 2–4 minutes to reheat. Serve immediately with a mixed salad.

* Crisp breadcrumbs, white, brown or wholemeal, make an attractive crunchy topping for many savoury dishes. Make the breadcrumbs in your food processor or liquidizer, using day-old bread. Then spread them on a baking sheet and dry them out in your *conventional* oven when you are going to use it anyway. Remove when crisp and brown, and cool and pack in rigid polythene containers. Keep in the fridge for up to two weeks.

RAISIN AND BANANA TEA BREAD

Cook the tea bread in a reusable 18cm (7in) microwave ring mould, available from most supermarkets and many stores. A high-fibre cake that may be served plain or spread with a little sugar-free jam if required.

PREPARATION TIME (after assembling ingredients):
10 minutes
MICROWAVE COOKING TIME: 9–10 minutes
SERVES: 6–8

150g (6oz) wholewheat
self-raising flour, sieved
with ½ × 5ml spoon (½
teaspoon) baking powder
150g (6oz) polyunsaturated
margarine
2–3 × 15ml spoons (2–3
tablespoons) semi-skimmed
milk

2 eggs, size 2
100g (4oz) soft light-brown
sugar
1 large ripe banana, sliced
75g (3oz) raisins

TO SERVE
1 banana
lemon juice

1. Very lightly grease a clear, reusable, fluted microwave ring
    mould.
2. Put the flour, margarine, milk, eggs and sugar into a mixing
    bowl and mix with an electric mixer until light and fluffy, or
    use a wooden spoon which will take just a little longer.
3. Fold in the raisins and banana – the mixture should be of a
    soft dropping consistency.
4. Turn into the prepared container and level the top.
5. Microwave, uncovered, on 70%/ROAST for 9–10 minutes, or
    until well risen and just set.
6. Allow to stand in the container for 20 minutes, then turn out
    on to a wire rack and allow to cool completely. Ease round
    the edge with a knife.
7. To serve, slice the remaining banana and brush the slices
    with a little lemon juice. Decorate the cake with the banana
    slices arranged, overlapping slightly, round the edge.

FISH CAKES

These healthy fish cakes are cooked on the browning dish. The
wheatgerm coating provides vitamin B while the fish provides
protein, vitamins and minerals, and the potatoes carbohydrate
and fibre. The children will love these crispy rounds of fish and
potatoes.

PREPARATION TIME (after assembling ingredients):
20 minutes
MICROWAVE COOKING TIME: 13½ minutes
SERVES: 4

350g (12oz) cod fillet
30ml (2 tablespoons)
   semi-skimmed milk
225g (8oz) potatoes, peeled
   and diced
1 × 15ml spoon (1 tablespoon)
   natural country bran
a little natural sea-salt
2 × 5ml spoons (2 teaspoons)
   tomato purée
1 × 5ml spoon (1 teaspoon)
   lemon juice

1 × 5ml spoon (1 teaspoon)
   dried oregano
freshly ground black pepper
1 egg, beaten
25g (1oz) Jordans
   natural   ⎫
   wheatgerm   ⎬ mix
50g (2oz) wholemeal ⎭ together
   breadcrumbs
1 × 15ml spoon (1 tablespoon)
   corn oil

1. Lay the fish in a dish. Pour over the milk, cover and microwave on 100%/FULL power for 5 minutes, or until the fish is cooked. Set aside, covered.

2. Put the potatoes into a medium-sized bowl. Add 2 × 15ml spoons (2 tablespoons) water. Cover and microwave on 100%/FULL power for 5 minutes, stir and stand for 5 minutes, then drain.

3. Mash the potatoes down. Flake in the fish with its juices, discarding the skin. Add the bran, tomato purée, lemon juice and oregano. Season with a little salt and pepper. Mix well to combine.

4. Turn the mixture on to a board and shape into 4 rounds – use a little wholewheat flour if necessary.

5. Pre-heat a large browning dish, without the lid, on 100%/FULL power for 7 minutes, or a small browning dish for 5 minutes.

6. Beat the egg in a cereal bowl and put the wheatgerm and breadcrumbs in another cereal bowl alongside.

7. Brush the fish cakes with the beaten egg and then coat them with the wheatgerm and breadcrumb mixture on all sides.

8. Pour the oil on to the hot dish, tipping the dish so that it coats the base. Put the fish cakes into the dish.

9. Microwave, uncovered, on 100%/FULL power for 2 minutes.

10. Turn over and continue to microwave on 100%/FULL power for 1½ minutes. Serve with peas and coleslaw.

* Microwave the peas before the fish cakes. One 275g (10oz) packet of frozen peas will take 5 minutes on 100%/FULL power. Simply pierce the packet once and lay it on two sheets of absorbent paper on a serving dish. Microwave on 100%/FULL power for 5 minutes, turning the bag over once half-way through the cooking time. Snip open the bag and turn into the dish. Carefully pull out the paper that will have protected your dish from becoming marked by the print on the packet; it will also have drained excess moisture from the peas. Set aside, covered, while cooking the fish cakes. It may be necessary to return the peas to the microwave for 1 minute, covered, before serving.

HONEY CUSTARDS

Easily digested and delicious warm or cold, these individual desserts use honey instead of the more traditional caramel base. A light-textured, high-protein pud.

PREPARATION TIME (after assembling ingredients):
    10 minutes
MICROWAVE COOKING TIME: 15 minutes
SERVES: 4

4 × 15ml (4 tablespoons) runny honey

450ml (¾ pint) semi-skimmed milk

4 large eggs, lightly beaten

a little ground allspice (optional)

1. Put 1 tablespoon of honey into each of four ramekins.

2. Combine the beaten eggs and milk in a jug and pass through a sieve.

3. Divide evenly between the ramekins. Sprinkle with allspice, if used.

4. Arrange in ring fashion in the microwave and cook, uncovered, on 50%/MEDIUM for about 15 minutes, or until set; rearrange the dishes twice during this time.

* I keep a tea-strainer especially for this recipe and simply hold it above each ramekin as I pour the milk and egg mixture through. Don't use the strainer you use for your tea!

5. Let stand for 10 minutes, then run a knife round the edges, turn out and serve warm. Can also be served cold.

POTATO AND CHICKEN SALAD

High-protein, low-fat chicken and high-fibre potatoes served in a creamy tomato mayonnaise. A balanced meal for children of all ages. Serve it on a bed of shredded lettuce, accompanied by a tomato and cucumber salad.

PREPARATION TIME (after assembling ingredients):
    5 minutes
MICROWAVE COOKING TIME: 12–14 minutes
SERVES: 4

3 chicken breast fillets, 125g (5oz) each
1 × 15ml spoon (1 tablespoon) lemon juice
a few snipped chives
450g (1lb) potatoes, scrubbed clean and roughly diced
2 × 15ml spoons (2 tablespoons) sweetcorn

1–2 cloves garlic, crushed (optional)
a little sea-salt
250ml (½ pint) corn oil
freshly ground black pepper
1 × 5ml spoon (1 teaspoon) tomato purée
2 × 15ml (2 tablespoons) natural yoghurt

FOR THE MAYONNAISE
1 egg, size 3
1 egg yolk

TO GARNISH
freshly snipped chives

1. Cook the chicken: Arrange the chicken breasts in a suitable shallow dish. Pour over the lemon juice and sprinkle with the chives. Cover and microwave on 100%/FULL power for 4–5 minutes. Set aside, covered, until cold.
2. Put the diced potatoes into a roasting bag. Add 2 × 15ml spoons (2 tablespoons) cold water. Stand the bag in a bowl or casserole. Seal the opening loosely with a rubber band.
3. Microwave on 100%/FULL power for 8–9 minutes, turning the bag over once after 4 minutes. Set aside for 5 minutes, then drain in a sieve and refresh under the cold tap. Drain on absorbent kitchen paper and turn into a 1.7 litre (3 pint) mixing-bowl.

179

4. Make the mayonnaise: Put the egg yolk and egg into a food processor or liquidizer (use the metal blade if you are using a food processor). Add the crushed garlic, if you are using it, a little sea-salt and a little freshly ground black pepper.
5. Process for about 5 seconds. With the machine running, gradually add the oil, very slowly at first and then a little faster, until the mayonnaise is thick and creamy.
6. Add the tomato purée with the natural yoghurt and process again, just to combine.
7. Cut the cold chicken into strips and mix in with the potatoes. Add the sweetcorn.
8. Pour the mayonnaise on to the potato and chicken and gently mix.
9. Turn on to a bed of shredded lettuce and serve, garnished with chives.

SPICY APPLE CAKE

Serve this spicy fruit cake hot as a pudding or cold at tea-time. Made with wholewheat flour and apples, it is high in fibre. The spices add flavour. This cake will keep well in an airtight tin.

PREPARATION TIME (after assembling ingredients): 12 minutes
MICROWAVE COOKING TIME: 20–22 minutes
SERVES: 6–8

225g (8oz) polyunsaturated margarine, at room temperature
225g (8oz) muscovado sugar
1 × 15ml spoon (1 tablespoon) runny honey, rounded
225g (8oz) wholewheat flour, self-raising
3 eggs, size 2
2–3 × 15ml spoons (2–3 tablespoons) milk

225g (8oz) Bramley cooking apples, peeled, cored and roughly chopped
2 × 5ml spoons (2 teaspoons) grated nutmeg
1 × 5ml spoon (1 teaspoon) ground cinnamon

TO SERVE
apple slices
lemon juice

1. Put the margarine and sugar into a large mixing bowl with the honey.
2. Cream together with a wooden spoon, or an electric mixer, until light and fluffy.
3. Beat in the eggs, one at a time. Beat in the milk.
4. Fold in the flour with the spices and the chopped apple.
5. Turn into a lightly oiled, Anchor Hocking, large microwave ring mould.
6. Microwave, uncovered, on 60%/MEDIUM for 20–22 minutes, or until well risen and set. It is advisable to give the dish a ¼-turn three times during cooking – don't worry about opening the door.
7. Allow to stand in the container for 20 minutes.
8. Turn out and serve warm or cold, decorated with slices of fresh apple that have been brushed with lemon juice.

CHEESY BAKED POTATOES

The microwave's ability to cook a jacket potato in 5 minutes makes them a wonderful standby when a quick healthy meal is called for. Mixed with sieved cottage cheese and grated Edam, these potatoes make a protein-packed meal that is low on fat and high on fibre.

PREPARATION TIME (after assembling ingredients):
  10 minutes
MICROWAVE COOKING TIME: 22 minutes
SERVES: 8 as a snack, or 4 as a complete meal

4 × 225g (8oz) potatoes, scrubbed clean
100g (4oz) cottage cheese
4 spring onions, chopped
1 × 15ml spoon (1 tablespoon) tomato ketchup
2 × 15ml spoons (2 tablespoons) semi-skimmed milk
75g (3oz) Edam cheese, grated

1. Prick the potatoes on all sides with a fork.
2. Stand on a dinner-plate, in ring fashion.
3. Microwave on 100%/FULL power for 18 minutes, turning each potato over once, half-way through the cooking time.

4. Wrap in a clean tea-towel and set aside for 10 minutes (the potatoes will continue to cook during this time).
5. Cut the potatoes in half and carefully scoop out the flesh, being careful not to damage the skins.
6. Mash the potato down in a medium bowl, adding the cottage cheese, spring onions, tomato sauce and semi-skimmed milk. Beat with a fork.
7. Fold in 50g (2oz) Edam.
8. Pile the mixture back into the potato shells. Arrange on a serving dish, sprinkle evenly with the remaining Edam, and microwave on 100%/FULL power for about 4 minutes to reheat and to melt the cheese.
9. Serve immediately with a crunchy coleslaw salad.

APPLE AND DATE DESSERT

Adding chopped, stoned dates to apples means that very little sweetener is required in this high-fibre, filling dessert. As an alternative, use chopped, dried apricots or raisins.

PREPARATION TIME (after assembling ingredients):
    10 minutes
MICROWAVE COOKING TIME: 7 minutes
SERVES: 4

675g (1½lb) Bramley cooking apples, peeled and thinly sliced

1 × 15ml spoon (1 tablespoon) runny honey
100g (4oz) stoned dates, chopped

1. Put the prepared Bramleys into a 1.7 litre (3 pint) casserole. Add the honey. Cover and microwave on 100%/FULL power for about 7 minutes, stirring and re-covering after 4 minutes.
2. Stir to ensure the apples have 'fallen'. If necessary, return to the microwave, covered, for 1–2 minutes. Stir in the dates.
3. Turn into individual serving dishes and serve cold.

* Wholewheat biscuits or sponge fingers can be served with this dessert.

INDEX

FOR THE BEST IN PAPERBACKS, LOOK FOR THE ⬤

In every corner of the world, on every subject under the sun, Penguin represents quality and variety – the very best in publishing today.

For complete information about books available from Penguin – including Pelicans, Puffins, Peregrines and Penguin Classics – and how to order them, write to us at the appropriate address below. Please note that for copyright reasons the selection of books varies from country to country.

In the United Kingdom: For a complete list of books available from Penguin in the U.K., please write to *Dept E.P., Penguin Books Ltd, Harmondsworth, Middlesex, UB7 0DA*

In the United States: For a complete list of books available from Penguin in the U.S., please write to *Dept BA, Penguin, 299 Murray Hill Parkway, East Rutherford, New Jersey 07073*

In Canada: For a complete list of books available from Penguin in Canada, please write to *Penguin Books Canada Ltd, 2801 John Street, Markham, Ontario L3R 1B4*

In Australia: For a complete list of books available from Penguin in Australia, please write to the *Marketing Department, Penguin Books Australia Ltd, P.O. Box 257, Ringwood, Victoria 3134*

In New Zealand: For a complete list of books available from Penguin in New Zealand, please write to the *Marketing Department, Penguin Books (NZ) Ltd, Private Bag, Takapuna, Auckland 9*

In India: For a complete list of books available from Penguin, please write to *Penguin Overseas Ltd, 706 Eros Apartments, 56 Nehru Place, New Delhi, 110019*

In Holland: For a complete list of books available from Penguin in Holland, please write to *Penguin Books Nederland B.V., Postbus 195, NL–1380AD Weesp, Netherlands*

In Germany: For a complete list of books available from Penguin, please write to *Penguin Books Ltd, Friedrichstrasse 10 – 12, D–6000 Frankfurt Main 1, Federal Republic of Germany*

In Spain: For a complete list of books available from Penguin in Spain, please write to *Longman Penguin España, Calle San Nicolas 15, E–28013 Madrid, Spain*

Jane Grigson's Vegetable Book   Jane Grigson

The ideal guide to the cooking of everything from artichoke to yams, written with her usual charm and depth of knowledge by 'the most engaging food writer to emerge during the last few years' – *The Times*

More Easy Cooking for One or Two   Louise Davies

This charming book, full of ideas and easy recipes, offers even the novice cook good wholesome food with the minimum of effort.

The Cuisine of the Rose   Mireille Johnston

Classic French cooking from Burgundy and Lyonnais, including the most succulent dishes of meat and fish bathed in pungent sauces of wine and herbs.

Good Food from Your Freezer   Helge Rubinstein and Sheila Bush

Using a freezer saves endless time and trouble and cuts your food bills dramatically; this book will enable you to cook just as well – perhaps even better – with a freezer as without.

An Invitation to Indian Cooking   Madhur Jaffrey

A witty, practical and delightful handbook of Indian cookery by the much loved presenter of the successful television series.

Budget Gourmet   Geraldene Holt

Plan carefully, shop wisely and cook well to produce first-rate food at minimal expense. It's as easy as pie!

FOR THE BEST IN PAPERBACKS, LOOK FOR THE

COOKERY IN PENGUINS

Mediterranean Food   Elizabeth David

Based on a collection of recipes made when the author lived in France, Italy, the Greek Islands and Egypt, this was the first book by Britain's greatest cookery writer.

The Complete Barbecue Book   James Marks

Mouth-watering recipes and advice on all aspects of barbecuing make this an ideal and inspired guide to *al fresco* entertainment.

A Book of Latin American Cooking   Elisabeth Lambert Ortiz

Anyone who thinks Latin American food offers nothing but *tacos* and *tortillas* will enjoy the subtle marriages of texture and flavour celebrated in this marvellous guide to one of the world's most colourful *cuisines*.

Quick Cook   Beryl Downing

For victims of the twentieth century, this book provides some astonishing gourmet meals – all cooked in under thirty minutes.

Josceline Dimbleby's Book of Puddings, Desserts and Savouries

'Full of the most delicious and novel ideas for every type of pudding' – *Lady*

Chinese Food   Kenneth Lo

A popular step-by-step guide to the whole range of delights offered by Chinese cookery and the fascinating philosophy behind it.

Audrey Eyton's F-Plus Audrey Eyton

'Your short-cut to the most sensational diet of the century' – *Daily Express*

Caring Well for an Older Person Muir Gray and Heather McKenzie

Wide-ranging and practical, with a list of useful addresses and contacts, this book will prove invaluable for anyone professionally concerned with the elderly or with an elderly relative to care for.

Baby and Child Penelope Leach

A beautifully illustrated and comprehensive handbook on the first five years of life. 'It stands head and shoulders above anything else available at the moment' – Mary Kenny in the *Spectator*

Woman's Experience of Sex Sheila Kitzinger

Fully illustrated with photographs and line drawings, this book explores the riches of women's sexuality at every stage of life. 'A book which any mother could confidently pass on to her daughter – and her partner too' – *Sunday Times*

Food Additives Erik Millstone

Eat, drink and be worried? Erik Millstone's hard-hitting book contains powerful evidence about the massive risks being taken with the health of consumers. It takes the lid off the food we eat and takes the lid off the food industry.

Pregnancy and Diet Rachel Holme

It *is* possible to eat well and healthily when pregnant while avoiding excessive calories; this book, with suggested foods, a sample diet-plan of menus and advice on nutrition, shows how.

PENGUIN HEALTH

Medicines: A Guide for Everybody   Peter Parish

This fifth edition of a comprehensive survey of all the medicines available over the counter or on prescription offers clear guidance for the ordinary reader as well as invaluable information for those involved in health care.

Pregnancy and Childbirth   Sheila Kitzinger

A complete and up-to-date guide to physical and emotional preparation for pregnancy – a must for all prospective parents.

The Penguin Encyclopaedia of Nutrition   John Yudkin

This book cuts through all the myths about food and diets to present the real facts clearly and simply. 'Everyone should buy one' – *Nutrition News and Notes*

The Parents' A to Z   Penelope Leach

For anyone with a child of 6 months, 6 years or 16 years, this guide to all the little problems involved in their health, growth and happiness will prove reassuring and helpful.

Jane Fonda's Workout Book

Help yourself to better looks, superb fitness and a whole new approach to health and beauty with this world-famous and fully illustrated programme of diet and exercise advice.

Alternative Medicine   Andrew Stanway

Dr Stanway provides an objective and practical guide to thirty-two alternative forms of therapy – from Acupuncture and the Alexander Technique to Macrobiotics and Yoga.